WHEN YO
TOGETHER

God's plans
for when his people meet
1 Corinthians 14:26

David Petts

Copyright © David Petts 2023

All Rights Reserved.

No part of this publication may be reproduced, stored in a retrieval system, or transmitted in any form or by any means – electronic, mechanical, photocopying, recording or otherwise – without prior permission from the author.

Published by www.davidpetts.org

ISBN 978-1-4477-7497-6

What then shall we say brothers and sisters? When you come together, everyone has a hymn, or a word of instruction, a revelation, a tongue or an interpretation. All of these must be done for the strengthening of the church (1 Corinthians 14:26).

What I am writing is the Lord's command (1 Corinthians 14:37).

About the author

David Petts grew up in a Christian home and gave his life to Christ at the age of fourteen, shortly after which he preached his first sermon. Now, seventy years later, he's still going strong.

After fifteen years in pastoral ministry, he served as Principal of Mattersey Hall Bible College from 1977 to 2004. He has also served as Chairman of the Executive Council of British Assemblies of God, President of the European Pentecostal Theological Association, Vice Chairman of the Pentecostal European Fellowship, and as a member of the Presidium of the Pentecostal World Fellowship.

His teaching ministry has taken him to over forty different countries where he has preached in churches, colleges, and universities around the world.

The author of several books, he has now made available over 200 podcasts, details of which may be found on his website.

A former Exhibitioner of Brasenose College, Oxford, David's academic achievements include an MA, an MTh, and a PhD in Theology. He is an Honorary Academic Fellow of the University of Wales.

He is married to Eileen who has been a strong support to his ministry for over 60 years. Their three children are all married and actively involved in Christian ministry.

Further information may be obtained from his website: www.davidpetts.org

CONTENTS

Author's preface: Why I have written this book 8

Introduction: 1 Corinthians 14:26 10

Ch. 1 Supernatural Gifts (12:1-11) 16

    These gifts are supernatural

    These gifts are for today

    These gifts are for us

Ch. 2 Baptism in the Spirit (12:13) 27

    Baptism in the Spirit in the book of Acts

    Baptism in the Spirit as the gateway to the gifts

    How Acts relates to 1 Corinthians 12:13

Ch. 3 Everybody's needed (12:12-30) 41

    The illustration of the human body (14-26)

    The illustration applied to the church (27-31)

    1 Corinthians 14:26 in the light of Chapter 12

Ch. 4 We're nothing without love (13:1-13) 51

    It's all meaningless without love (1-3)

    The nature of love (4-8)

    Recognising our limitations (8-12)

Ch. 5 Speaking in Tongues in Chapter 14 61

    How does Paul describe speaking in tongues?

    What is the purpose of speaking in tongues?

    How is speaking in tongues to be used in church?

Ch. 6 Interpretation of Tongues in Chapter 14 73

    References to interpretation of tongues

    Practical issues that arise from this

    A personal testimony

Ch. 7 Prophecy in Chapter 14 84

    What is prophecy?

    The value and purpose of prophecy

    The use of prophecy in church

Ch. 8 Identifying Underlying Principles 96

    Participation

    Variety

    Edification

Ch. 9 Putting it all into practice 110

    Being fully persuaded in your own mind

    Praying for guidance

    Consulting your fellow leaders

    Teaching the people

    Making space

    Creating a suitable environment

    Conclusion

AUTHOR'S PREFACE

Why I have written this book

In the seventy years I have been a Christian I have experienced church worship in numerous nations and different denominations, from the dignified formality of Anglo-Catholic services to the exuberant enthusiasm of African Pentecostalism. I have often heard it said that it's good that there are many different styles of worship because what suits one person may not suit another. But this places the emphasis on the preferences of the worshipper and ignores the possible preferences of the One who is being worshipped.

So the question arises, *Does God have anything to say about how he wants to be worshipped?* And, as a Bible believing Christian, I'm convinced that he does. I have been teaching and conducting seminars for national and international church leaders on this subject over the past three decades and have for some time felt that I should write a book on it.

What finally spurred me into action was the COVID pandemic. Church, for many people, changed quite a lot between 2020 and 2023. Christians around the world were challenged by the restrictions placed upon them imposed by government, and church leaders have been asking if God is trying to show us a better way of 'doing church'.

This in itself is a challenge, as many older Christians, like myself, have come to love many of the things we used to do, and the older you get, the harder it is to adapt to change. But it's always appropriate to take a look at the way we do things and ask ourselves if we could do better – or, more importantly, whether what we do is actually what God would want – whether what we are doing is *biblical*.

This book is written from the understanding that God's will is revealed in his word, the Bible. It's based on the assumption that in the Bible God has something to say about how we should worship him, and the kind of things we should expect to happen when we gather in Jesus' name.

It's not my intention to tell church leaders how they should do things. But I do believe that God's word teaches us clear principles about what should happen when Christians come together, and it is those principles that I'm seeking to underline and clarify. How they are worked out in practice in any local situation will be for leaders prayerfully to consider.

Finally, I am aware that what I have written may raise many questions. Some of these I have attempted to anticipate and to answer. Others I have not attempted to answer, partly because the purpose of this book is very specific, and partly because my answers are readily available in the books that are briefly described on pages 121-122.

For example, in Chapter One I stress the importance of supernatural gifts, and why we should expect them in our meetings. But there is much more that could be said about them which is beyond the scope and purpose of this book. However, I have written extensively about them in *Body Builders – Gifts to make God's people grow,* which I would encourage those who have further questions to read.

David Petts

Brixham, Devon, April 2023.

INTRODUCTION

1 Corinthians 14:26

Some readers may be surprised to know that the Bible does give us clear guidelines as to what should happen when Christians come together. In I Corinthians 14:26 the apostle Paul writes:

> ***What then shall we say*** *brothers and sisters? When you come together, everyone has a hymn, or a word of instruction, a revelation, a tongue or an interpretation. All of these must be done for the strengthening of the church.*

This verse is both a recognition and a recommendation – a recognition of what was already happening, and a recommendation that, whatever that was, it should be done for the strengthening of the church. The evidence that the verse contains a recommendation is the use of the phrase *What then shall we say...?* The same Greek phrase[1] is used in verse 15 where Paul is clearly encouraging the Corinthians to follow his example:

> ***So what shall I do?*** *I will pray with my spirit, but I will also pray with my mind; I will sing with my spirit, but I will also sing with my mind.*

So it seems reasonable to conclude that he's using it in the same way in verse 26. Indeed, in verse 37 he tells them that the things he is writing to them are *the Lord's command:*

---

[1] *ti oun estin.* Literally, *What is it, therefore?*

> *If anybody thinks he is a prophet or spiritually gifted, let him acknowledge that **what I am writing to you is the Lord's command.***

This strong statement must surely alert the attention of every Bible believing Christian to the fact that God cares very much about what we do when we come together. If God is worth worshipping at all – and he certainly is – shouldn't we do all we can to be sure that we're doing it *his* way?

So, verse 26 deserves our serious attention. It contains several underlying principles which are, I believe, vital for us to understand and apply to the way we do church, whatever the sociological or cultural situation in which we may find ourselves. And it's those principles that this book is seeking to emphasise.

But first, what does Paul mean when he says, *When you come together?* He is undoubtedly referring to the occasions when the Corinthians gathered as a church. This is clear from verse 23:

> *So if **the whole church comes together** and everyone speaks in tongues, and some who do not understand or some unbelievers come in, will they not say that you are out of your mind?*

Notice, too, verse 19:

> *But **in the church** I would rather speak five intelligible words to instruct others than ten thousand words in a tongue.*

Of course, by *in the church* he is not referring to a church building. At the time of writing the epistle (AD 53-54) there were no church buildings, and the Corinthians were almost certainly meeting in the homes of one or more of the members. This means that the numbers in the gathering would inevitably be smaller than those in some churches today. Paul's teaching can be made to work well in a relatively small church or in a home group, but perhaps not so easily in a larger church.

But does this mean that larger churches have nothing to learn from Paul's teaching in verse 26? By no means. The basic **principles** underlying Paul's teaching are relevant to all churches, and even larger churches can and should organise smaller gatherings where that teaching can be followed more easily. But we will return to this subject later in the book, after we have considered the implications of the verse in more detail.

The first principle we find in the verse is **participation**. Everybody is needed. Paul says, *every one of you has…* Perhaps we need to ask ourselves how many people are really *involved* in our meetings – or is their involvement limited to joining in the singing or saying *Amen* to the prayers? This is clearly not what Paul had in mind.

The second principle is **variety.** In 1 Corinthians 12:13-30 Paul teaches that every member of the body is different from the others, but every member is important. Here, in 14:26, that variety is expressed as the members gather together. One may bring *a hymn,* another *a word of instruction,* another *a revelation,* another *a tongue,* and another *an interpretation.*

Although these are presumably representative of the many different ways that Christians may contribute to the worship of the church, we see at least three important ingredients that Paul expects in our meetings:

- the musical dimension – *a hymn*
- the doctrinal dimension – *a word of instruction*
- the supernatural dimension – *a revelation, a tongue, or an interpretation.*

In my experience of Christian worship in over 40 different countries around the world there is no lack of the musical. In many, though by no means all, there is usually adequate scope for the doctrinal. But sadly, in many there is little manifestation of the supernatural. Even some churches that profess to believe in these things make little room for the miraculous gifts of the Holy Spirit in their meetings.

But it's clear that Paul expects to see the supernatural in the church. In 1 Corinthians 3:16 he teaches that the gathered church is the temple of the Holy Spirit. In Ephesians 2:21-22 it's *a holy temple in the Lord… a dwelling in which God lives by his Spirit.* And it's the presence of God's Spirit among us that makes the miraculous possible when we meet.

The third key principle is **edification**. Paul says *all these must be done for the strengthening of the church.* In chapter 13 he has taught the Corinthians that, whatever gifts we may have, if they are not motivated by love, they are of no value at all. And if we love people we will want to bless them. We want to edify them. That is, to see them built up in their faith. Whatever takes place must be for the strengthening of the church.

So the kind of meeting Paul is envisaging is one where every person gathered has opportunity to contribute something as they are led and empowered by the Holy Spirit. That contribution may come in a rich variety of ways, but whatever it may be, it must be motivated by love and the desire to be a blessing to others.

The three principles we have outlined from 1 Corinthians 14:26, **participation, variety, and edification**, in many ways summarise Paul's overall teaching on public worship contained in chapters 11-14.

We see the principle of **participation** in his teaching on the right use of spiritual gifts in chapters 12 and 14.

The principle of **variety** is vividly illustrated in 12:13-30 where Paul's theme is unity and diversity, and where he demonstrates our dependence on each other as members of the body of Christ.

And his wonderful teaching on love in chapter 13 leads us into the understanding in chapter 14 that the best way to show love is to put others first by seeking their **edification**, rather than just seeking a blessing for ourselves.

But underlying these principles is one that is even more important – **the leading and power of the Holy Spirit**. It's the Spirit who must enable our participation. It's the Spirit who brings variety to our meetings. And it's the Spirit who inspires us with words that will bring edification to the church. In 1 Corinthians 12:13 Paul refers to the baptism in the Holy Spirit, and we'll devote a chapter to discussing what it is and its relationship to the supernatural gifts of the Spirit.

So as we come to consider these themes in more detail, we'll be exploring chapters 12-14 in order to gain a fuller understanding of what he is saying in 1 Corinthians 14:26. As we do so, we'll discover, among other things, that:

- There's a supernatural dimension to the worship of the church expressed in the manifestation of supernatural gifts given by the Holy Spirit (12:1-11).

- These all spring from our being baptised in the Spirit (12:13).

- The church is the body of Christ, and every member of the body is different, and everybody is needed (12:12-30).

- Everything we do must be motivated by love (13:1-13).

- As an expression of that love, we must always seek to put other people first (14:1-25).

- This will mean using correctly the spiritual gifts God has given us by taking responsibility for our actions (14:26-40).

- In everything we must submit to the authority of scripture (14:37).

And when we've completed our study of these chapters we'll conclude with a chapter on the role of church leaders in seeking to implement Paul's teaching in the church today.

CHAPTER ONE

Supernatural Gifts

1 Corinthians 12:1-11

As we've already seen from what he says in 1 Corinthians 14:26, Paul certainly expected manifestations of the supernatural in the meetings of the church. He refers to *a revelation, a tongue, or an interpretation.* But these are by no means the only expressions of the supernatural power of the Holy Spirit. In 12:8-10 Paul mentions nine gifts:

> *a message of wisdom, a message of knowledge, faith, gifts of healing, miraculous powers, prophecy, distinguishing between spirits, speaking in tongues, interpretation of tongues.*

In Chapters 5-7 we'll be discussing tongues, interpretation and prophecy in more detail, as these are the gifts Paul concentrates on in 1 Corinthians 14. And because I have already written at length on spiritual gifts in *Body Builders*, in this chapter I will restrict myself to three major factors that are of immediate relevance to how we do church today. We will see that:

- These gifts are supernatural
- These gifts are for today
- These gifts are for us.

These gifts are supernatural

As we look at the immediate context in which these verses are set, we find strong evidence that Paul intends us to understand that all these gifts are supernatural. In verse 1 he tells the Corinthians that he does not want them to be ignorant about spiritual gifts. His usual word for any gift that God may give us is *charisma*, something which comes from his grace (*charis*). But here he uses the word *pneumatika*. This may well indicate that the gifts he has in mind are a unique form of *charisma*. All God's gifts, whether natural or supernatural, are *charismata*, but only the gifts in these verses are referred to as *pneumatika*. And verses 2-3 indicate that it's supernatural gifts that Paul has in mind:

> *You know that when you were pagans, somehow or other you were influenced and led astray to mute idols. Therefore I tell you that no one who is speaking by the Spirit of God says, "Jesus be cursed," and no one can say, "Jesus is Lord," except by the Holy Spirit.*

Before their conversion the Corinthians were idol-worshippers. This meant that they had been involved in devil-worship. This is clear from 10:19-20 where Paul says:

> *Do I mean then that a sacrifice offered to an idol is anything, or that an idol is anything? No, but the sacrifices of pagans are offered to demons, not to God, and I do not want you to be participants with demons.*

The confession that JESUS IS LORD is what marks a person as a Christian. In Romans 10:9 Paul says that:

> *... if you confess with your mouth, "**Jesus is Lord**," and believe in your heart that God raised him from the dead, you will be saved.*

As Christians, the people in Corinth to whom Paul was writing acknowledged the Lordship of Jesus. So there is no suggestion that they would have manifested demonic gifts, for *no one can say, "Jesus is Lord," except by the Holy Spirit* (v3). But people who were not yet believers and were still worshipping idols could come into their meetings (cf. 14:23) and might well do so.

It was therefore vitally important that Paul's readers should understand how to distinguish between divine and devilish manifestations. And it's just as important today. Demons do not acknowledge the Lordship of Jesus, as I once experienced during an encounter with a witch in Chester[2].

Furthermore, unlike demonic manifestations, where different gifts come from different spirits, in Christian worship the different gifts all come from the same Spirit:

> *There are **different kinds of gifts**, but **the same Spirit**. There are **different kinds of service**, but **the same Lord**. There are **different kinds of working**, but **the same God** works all of them in all men* (vv.4-6)[3].

Paul draws attention to the many **different** gifts and ministries in the church and points out that they all have their origin in **the same God**. The reference to the Trinity in these verses is interesting. Paul seems to be suggesting that the unity and diversity in the Godhead is

---

[2] See *Body Builders – Gifts to make God's people grow*, pp,240-243.
[3] Notice also the repeated reference to *the same Spirit* in verses 8-11.

reflected by a similar unity amid diversity in the church, a theme he is to develop later in the chapter.

So, from the context which immediately precedes the list of gifts in verses 8-10, it seems likely that Paul intends each of these gifts as a supernatural manifestation of the Holy Spirit, but he does not define them. This suggests that the Corinthians obviously knew what they were. In fact, in 1:7 we read that the Corinthians did not lack any spiritual gift. They knew what they were – indeed they had received them and were using them – but their ignorance lay in the fact that they did not use them correctly.

In the following four paragraphs I have given what I consider to be the most likely definition or description of each gift, but for a more sophisticated analysis please consult what I have said in *Body Builders*[4].

I have rejected the view that, although most of the gifts in this list are miraculous, **a message of wisdom and a message of knowledge** are simply the ability to speak with wisdom and knowledge. It seems to me far more likely that, although we may not be certain about exactly what Paul had in mind, he intends us to understand them as some form of supernatural revelation[5].

As far as the remaining gifts in the list are concerned, what Paul means is fairly clear. **Faith** is the miracle working faith that can move mountains (cf.13:2). **Gifts of healing** are miraculous healings performed without medical aid. **Miraculous powers** are, by

---

[4] *Body Builders – Gifts to make God's people grow,* Part Two,
[5] For detailed discussion on the nature of these two gifts, see *Body Builders* pp. 247-269.

definition, miraculous, and probably include miracles that do not come under the category of gifts of healing.

Prophecy, which is to be distinguished from prediction on the one hand and preaching on the other, brings by inspiration of the Spirit words of edification, encouragement, and comfort to the church (14:3). **Distinguishing between spirits** probably refers to discerning whether a supernatural occurrence is motivated by the Holy Spirit or by an evil spirit, or detecting the presence of evil spirits where their activity might not otherwise be obvious.

Speaking in tongues is speaking a language one has never learned, as the disciples did on the day of Pentecost (Acts 2), and **interpretation of tongues** is the ability imparted by the Spirit to interpret what has been spoken in tongues.

Assuming that these definitions are broadly correct, we see that both the contents of the list and the context in which it is set confirm the view that these gifts are all supernatural. This is further confirmed in verse 13 by Paul's reference to the baptism in the Holy Spirit which we will consider in the next chapter.

But even if it were true that *some* of these gifts were not supernatural, our contention that we should expect the supernatural in our meetings would still hold good. Because, as we have seen, in 14:26 Paul mentions supernatural gifts like tongues and interpretation as part of what can be expected in our meetings.

These gifts are for today

People who believe that the supernatural gifts of the Spirit are not for today are known as cessationists. Perhaps the most common version of cessationism is the view that these gifts were withdrawn once the writing of the New Testament was complete.

Obviously, if they are right about this, then my view that 1 Corinthians 14:26 gives us direction as to what should happen in church today is entirely wrong. But that would make much of what Paul says in chapters 12-14 irrelevant for the church today, and, for that matter, for the church of the last nineteen centuries!

However, the cessationist view has no solid basis in scripture. The verses that are usually quoted to support their view are 1 Corinthians 13:8-10, where we read:

> *Love never fails. But where there are prophecies, they will cease; where there are tongues, they will be stilled; where there is knowledge, it will pass away. For we know in part and we prophesy in part, but when perfection comes, the imperfect disappears.*

Cessationists claim that gifts like prophecy and tongues have ceased because they believe that *perfection* (v10) came once the Bible was complete. But do they really believe that knowledge has also passed away? And a look at the context quickly reveals that their view is misguided. This is clear from what he says in verse 12:

> *Now we see but a poor reflection as in a mirror; then we shall see face to face. Now I know in part; then I shall know fully, even as I am fully known.*

Paul is looking far beyond the completion of the New Testament. *Perfection* will come when he sees Jesus *face to face.* What he sees *now* is only *a poor reflection* of what he will see *then. Then* he will know him completely – *fully.* This must surely refer to when he sees Jesus in heaven, where tongues and prophecy will not be needed, and ultimately to the return of the Lord at the end of the age. Indeed, Paul strongly implies this when he says in 1 Corinthians 1:7 that the Corinthians *do not lack **any** spiritual gift as* they *eagerly wait for our Lord Jesus Christ to be revealed.* He clearly expected the gifts to be in evidence until the second coming of Christ.

Finally, the cessationist position does not stand up in the light of present-day Christian experience. For example, there are numerous well documented cases of speaking in tongues being recognised as it was at Pentecost by hearers who recognised it as their own native language[6]. Such miracles can only spring from one of two sources – the divine or the demonic. But Christians who speak in tongues gladly acknowledge the Lordship of Jesus, and that, as we have seen, is the biblical test of that which is truly divine.

These gifts are for us

So far we have seen that the gifts listed in 1 Corinthians 12:8-10 are all supernatural, that they are for today, and that we should expect the supernatural in our meetings (14:26). But can we expect **all** these gifts? The answer to this question in any particular situation will depend on two main factors – divine sovereignty and human responsibility.

---

[6] See, for example, Harris, R.W., *Spoken by the Spirit,* GPH, Springfield MO, 1973. See also my personal testimony on pages 84-86 and in *Body Builders* pp.149-151.

In 1 Corinthians 12:11 Paul tells us that

> *All these are the work of one and the same Spirit, and he gives them to each one, just as he determines.*

This means that the Holy Spirit decides what gifts he will give to any individual Christian. He knows what's best for us as individuals. But he also knows what's best for the church. And no two churches are alike. It follows, therefore, that the gifts manifested in a local church at any given time will be distributed by the Spirit in accordance with the needs of that particular church, because the purpose of every gift is the good of the church:

> *Now to each one the manifestation of the Spirit is given* **for the common good** (12:7).

This theme is picked up in 14:1-5 where Paul says that prophecy is to be preferred to speaking in tongues, because uninterpreted tongues only edifies the speaker, but prophecy edifies the church. The gifts are given **to** individuals, but they're **for the benefit of** the whole church[7].

So the gifts are given at the discretion of the Holy Spirit. But that does not mean that we have no responsibility in this matter. It's our responsibility to *follow the way of love and* ***eagerly desire*** *spiritual gifts* (14:1).

In some churches there is little or no desire for these gifts simply because they know little about them. This is because their leaders never teach about them, perhaps because they are not sufficiently

---

[7] Correctly understood, 1 Corinthians 12:13 also illustrates this principle. See Chapter Two.

confident in their own understanding to encourage them. I will be saying more about this in the final chapter of this book, but at this stage it's enough to note that we can't expect these gifts in our meetings if there's no desire for them.

But in churches where there is a desire and where the members are encouraged to be filled with the Spirit, it's safe to assume that at least some of these gifts will be manifested. If the word of God tells us to *eagerly desire spiritual gifts* then we can be sure that God wants us to have them. As we have already seen, 1 Corinthians 14:26 encourages the use of gifts like tongues and interpretation in our meetings, and 14:1 especially mentions prophecy as a gift to be eagerly desired. And although it would probably be wrong to suggest that these gifts should be in evidence in every meeting, we need to remember that Paul did recommend their use **when** *you come together* (14:26)[8].

But what about other gifts like healing, for example? We certainly cannot say that they cannot be used in the context of the gathered church, during a time of 'prayer ministry' for example, for all the gifts are given for the benefit of the church (12:7). But it is evident from Mark 16 and the book of Acts that gifts like healing and miracles were very much used in evangelism which usually took place outside and not in a meeting where the church had gathered for worship.

I have no wish to be dogmatic on this matter, but in my view, although miraculous gifts like healing may well be expected in evangelistic meetings held in churches, from a New Testament

---

[8] It's noteworthy that *hotan*, the Greek word used here for *when,* can also carry the sense of *whenever*.

perspective they would be more effective when used out on the streets, as was most often the case in the book of Acts.

If this view is correct, it's possible that in 14:26, when talking of supernatural gifts, Paul restricts himself to mentioning those that are usually to be expected in a church meeting. So we should not be surprised if gifts like prophecy, tongues, and interpretation are the gifts that are in greater evidence in our meetings today. But that by no means precludes the possibility of other gifts being manifested as the Holy Spirit determines.

Conclusion

In this chapter we have seen that:

- God does not want us to be ignorant about spiritual gifts.
- The gifts listed in 1 Corinthians 12:8-10 are supernatural.
- Not all supernatural manifestations come from the Holy Spirit. The test that a gift has genuinely come from God is the confession that Jesus is Lord.
- Although there is a rich variety of supernatural gifts, each gift is given by the same Spirit.
- The gifts are given, as the Holy Spirit determines, to individual Christians for the benefit of the whole church.
- The view that these gifts were withdrawn once the writing of the New Testament was complete is entirely mistaken.
- These gifts are for today and we should expect them to be regularly in evidence in our meetings.

- Where they are not in evidence, this may well be caused by lack of desire, possibly due to a lack of teaching or encouragement on the part of church leaders (especially those who hold a cessationist view).

Finally, two more things should be added:

- Although in this chapter we have stressed the supernatural, our natural gifts and talents are also important. All God's gracious gifts are needed, whether natural or supernatural. While we shouldn't minimise the importance of natural gifts, we must not content ourselves solely with them, given God's generosity in giving the supernatural to us,

- However much of the supernatural we experience there will always be unanswered questions. We know in part, and we prophesy in part. Who knows why Peter was supernaturally delivered from prison while Stephen was stoned to death and James was beheaded? Questions like these may never be answered until that day when we *know fully*, even as we are fully known. Until then, we walk by faith and not by sight, and we must continue to expect the miraculous gifts of the Spirit to be manifest in our lives and in our meetings.

CHAPTER TWO

Baptism the Spirit

1 Corinthians 12:13

We have seen from 1 Corinthians 14:26 that among the things that Paul tells us to expect in our meetings are supernatural gifts like speaking in tongues and interpretation. We saw too that the gifts that Paul mentions in 1 Corinthians 12:1-11 are all supernatural. Such manifestations would clearly be impossible if it were not for the inspiration of the Holy Spirit. So it's not surprising that in these verses there are no less than eight references to the Holy Spirit.

It's only by the Holy Spirit that we can confess that Jesus is Lord (3). Although we have different gifts, it's the same Spirit that inspires them all (4). If we have received a gift from the Spirit, it's not for our benefit alone, but for the good of all the church (7). All these supernatural gifts are given by *the same Spirit* who gives them to each one, *just as he determines* (8-11). It's clear, then, that if we are to see these gifts in operation in our meetings, we need the presence and power of the Spirit moving among us.

But what exactly does Paul mean in verse 13 when he talks about being baptised *by* or *in* the Spirit? Different versions translate this verse in a variety of ways, and this has led to several different interpretations, none of which is entirely satisfactory. But bearing in mind the context in which the verse is set and the Greek terminology used by Paul, I have translated the first part of the verse as follows:

> *For we have all been baptised* **in** *one Spirit* **for** *(the purpose or benefit of) one body.*

I have written at length elsewhere giving detailed reasons for this translation[9], so here I will keep my explanation relatively brief. First, I have translated the Greek word *en* as *in*, because, although it can mean *by*, its usual meaning is *in*. This is the same Greek preposition as is used in Acts 1:5 when Jesus says:

> *...in a few days you will be baptised in the Holy Spirit.*

This identifies what Paul is talking about in 1 Corinthians 12:13 with the baptism in the Spirit Jesus spoke about when he promised the disciples that they would soon receive power to be his witnesses when the Holy Spirit came upon them (Acts 1:8).

And secondly, I have translated the Greek word *eis* as **for**, because although it can mean *into*, this is by no means its only meaning. Consider the following example which I have chosen simply because it contains no less than three different uses of the word *eis*:

> *When Jesus had called the Twelve together, he gave them power and authority to drive out all demons and to cure diseases, 2 and he sent them out to preach the kingdom of God and to heal the sick. 3 He told them: "Take nothing **for the journey** – no staff, no bag, no bread, no money, no extra tunic. 4 **Whatever house you enter**, stay there until you leave that town. 5 If people do not welcome you, shake the dust off your feet when you leave their town, **as a testimony against***

---

[9] For further discussion of this theme, see my article *Baptism in the Spirit in Pauline Thought* in JEPTA, Vol. 7, No.3, p. 98ff. See also my article in *Pentecostal Perspectives*, K. Warrington (Ed), Paternoster, 1998, p98ff. See also *The Holy Spirit – an Introduction*, pages 87-90.

***them**." 6 So they set out and went from village to village, preaching the gospel and healing people everywhere.*

This is the NIV translation of Luke 9:1-6. I have emphasised the three places where Luke uses *eis*. In verse 3 Jesus tells his disciples to take nothing **for** the journey. So *eis* here means *for*. It conveys the idea of *purpose*. In verse 4, a literal translation would be, ***into** whatever house you enter*. So here *eis* means *into*. And in verse 5 *eis* is translated as *as,* but this could equally well have been translated as *for*. Replace *as* with the word *for* and it means exactly the same. Again, it conveys the idea of *purpose*.

So, bearing this in mind, 1 Corinthians 12:13 could well mean

*For we have all been baptised **in** one Spirit **for** (the purpose or benefit of) one body*

as I have suggested. What's more, from the context of the supernatural gifts in which it is set, it's clear to me that the verse is best understood to refer to the baptism in the Spirit that was promised by Jesus in Acts 1:5, received by the disciples on the day of Pentecost, and described by Luke in subsequent chapters of Acts.

So in the rest of this chapter we'll be considering what Acts reveals about what it means to be baptised in the Spirit, why we should understand baptism in the Spirit to be the gateway to the supernatural gifts of the Spirit, and how this relates to our understanding of 1 Corinthians 12:13.

Baptism in the Spirit in the book of Acts

In 1 Corinthians 12:13 Paul does not *define* baptism in the Spirit. This is almost certainly because he knows that the Corinthians will understand his terminology. He is using their knowledge of an experience with which they were already familiar to *illustrate* the unity of the body of Christ. So for us to understand what he means by baptism in the Spirit we need to turn to the book of Acts which often describes experiences referred to in the epistles and helps us understand them.

To begin with, it will be helpful to understand that although Acts contains only two references to the words, *You will be baptised in the Holy Spirit*[10], it's clear that Luke uses a variety of expressions to refer to the same experience. These include:

- Receiving the gift the Father had promised (1:4)
- Being baptised in the Holy Spirit (1:5)
- The power of the Spirit coming or falling on you (1:8, 8:16, 10:44)
- Being filled with the Spirit (2:4)
- Receiving (the gift of) the Holy Spirit (2:38, 8:15, 8:17, 8:19, 10:47, 19:2).

All these expressions are references to the baptism in the Spirit and teach us something about it. For example, in Acts 1:5 Jesus said:

> *Do not leave Jerusalem, but wait for the gift my Father promised, which you have heard me speak about. For John baptised with water, but in a few days **you will be baptised in the Holy Spirit**'...*

He goes on to clarify its meaning in Acts 1:8 when he says:

---

[10] Acts 1:5 and Acts 11:16 where Peter quotes the words of Jesus and applies them to the experience of Cornelius.

> ...*you will receive power when the Holy Spirit comes on you; and you will be my witnesses in Jerusalem, and in all Judea and Samaria, and to the ends of the earth.*

And the power they were to receive from the Spirit was supernatural, miracle-working power, as the opening verses of Acts 2 make clear:

> *When the day of Pentecost came, they were all together in one place. Suddenly a sound like the blowing of a violent wind came from heaven and filled the whole house where they were sitting. They saw what seemed to be tongues of fire that separated and came to rest on each of them.* ***All of them were filled with the Holy Spirit and began to speak in other tongues as the Spirit enabled them*** (Acts 2:1-4).

The promise that Jesus had made them was fulfilled. He had told them to wait for the gift that God had promised (Acts 1:4) and that they would be baptised in the Holy Spirit (Acts 1:5). This would be the power of the Holy Spirit coming on them empowering them to be witnesses to the ends of the earth (Acts 1:8). And this happened on the day of Pentecost when the disciples were filled with the Holy Spirit and began to speak languages they had never learned (Acts 2:4). So Luke uses all these different expressions to refer to the same experience.

As a result of this amazing miracle, a large crowd gathered and, after Peter had preached the gospel to them, over 3000 people were added to the church. Acts goes on to tell us how, through the power of the Holy Spirit, thousands more people became Christians and churches were established throughout the then-known world.

But there's more that we can learn from Acts about what it means to be baptised in the Spirit. Please note carefully the following points:

- It's different from becoming a Christian.

- It's different from sanctification.

- It's a supernatural experience.

- It's available to every Christian in every generation.

It's different from becoming a Christian

The first thing to notice is that when the disciples were filled with the Spirit on the day of Pentecost they were *already* followers of Jesus. Their experience of the Spirit that day was not what made them Christians. They had already left all to follow Jesus (Matthew 19:27). They had confessed that he was the Christ, the Son of the living God (Matthew 16:16). He had told them that they were already clean (John 15:3) and that their names were written in Heaven (Luke 10:20). But until Pentecost they were not yet baptised in the Spirit.

We see something similar when we look at the Samaritans who were converted through Philip's preaching in Acts 8. They had believed Philip as he had preached the gospel to them and they had been baptised (v. 12), but the Holy Spirit had not yet *come upon* any of them (v. 16). However, when Peter and John placed their hands on them (v.17), they *received* the Holy Spirit.

Other examples in Acts are the apostle Paul who was converted on the road to Damascus but was not filled with the Spirit until Ananias had laid his hands on him (Acts 9:3-17), and the Ephesians in Acts 19:1-6. The Spirit came on them *after* Paul had laid hands on them, *after* he had baptised them in water, *after* he had explained to them that it was Jesus who was the Christ about whom John the Baptist had told them. (Note, too, from the examples we have mentioned that the baptism in the Spirit was often received through the laying on of hands, but the New Testament never teaches this as a means of receiving salvation).

All these examples show us that, when Luke uses expressions like *being baptised in the Spirit, being filled with the Spirit, receiving the Spirit, the Spirit coming upon a person,* he is not talking about the work of the Holy Spirit in our lives which brings about our conversion. Being baptised in the Spirit is different from being born again[11].

It's different from sanctification

The next thing to notice from the Book of Acts is that being baptised in the Spirit is not the same as sanctification. It's something that happens suddenly. Let's go back to the first few verses of Acts 2. For ten days the disciples had been waiting for the coming of the Holy Spirit. They were no more filled with the Spirit on the ninth day than they had been on the first day! But on the tenth day, the day of Pentecost, they were *suddenly* (v2) *filled with the Spirit* (v4). This is clear from the use of the word *suddenly* in verse 2 and from the tense of the Greek verb which Luke uses in verse 4. And the same is true of the verb used in Acts 4:31 when the disciples were filled again with the Holy Spirit[12].

Other examples in Acts include Acts 1:5 where Jesus promises his disciples that they will be *baptised* in the Holy Spirit and Peter's statement in Acts 11:15 that the Holy Spirit *fell on* Cornelius[13]. Falling

---

[11] I have written in more detail on this in *The Holy Spirit – an Introduction*. For more details, please see the books listed at the back of this book.

[12] The verb 'filled' is in the Aorist Tense which is 'strictly the expression of a momentary or transient, single action' (Analytical Greek Lexicon, Bagster).

[13] The Greek verb means 'fell on' rather than 'came on' as in NIV.

seems to suggest something that happens suddenly and baptism – always by immersion in the New Testament – should certainly not be administered gradually!

This is important because some Christians have mistakenly confused being filled with the Spirit with the gradual process of sanctification that takes place in our lives day by day as we seek to become more like Jesus. So, being baptised in the Spirit is a sudden experience that's not to be confused with regeneration[14] or with sanctification. But it's also important to understand that it's a supernatural experience.

It's a supernatural experience

We only need to read Acts 2:1-4 again to see that being baptised with the Spirit is a supernatural experience. They saw supernatural tongues of fire, heard the supernatural wind of the Spirit, and spoke by supernatural power languages they had never learned. In Acts there is a clear connection between the initial experience of the baptism in the Spirit and speaking in tongues (Acts 2:4, 10:46, 19:6).

In fact, wherever there is a full description of people being baptised in Spirit, the first thing to be recorded immediately afterwards is that those who received the Spirit spoke in tongues (Acts 2:4, 10:46, 19:6). In Acts 10:46, for example, it was how Peter and his companions knew that the new converts in Cornelius's household had been baptised in the Spirit.

---

[14] Although it may, as is clearly the case with Cornelius and his household, happen on the same occasion (Acts 10).

But their experience of the Spirit was not to be limited to speaking in tongues. The baptism in the Spirit accompanied by speaking in tongues was only the gateway to other mighty gifts. As we read on in Acts we see that by the same supernatural power of the Spirit they healed the sick (Chapters 3, 5, 8, 9, 14, 19, 28), cast out demons (Chapters 8, 16, 19) and even raised the dead (Chapters 9 and 20). As a result, thousands were added to the church (Acts 2:41, 4:4).

So Acts paints a picture of the baptism in the Spirit as a supernatural experience, which leads to further manifestations of the miraculous which confirm the preaching of the gospel and result in the formation of churches. And these things were not just for the early disciples.

It's available to every Christian in every generation

This is made clear in Acts 2:38-39 where Peter says to the crowd:

> *Repent and be baptised, every one of you, in the name of Jesus Christ for the forgiveness of your sins. And you will receive the gift of the Holy Spirit. The promise is for you and your children and for all who are far off – for all whom the Lord our God will call.*

The gift of the Holy Spirit is available to all who will repent and be baptised. It was not just for those Peter was speaking to in Acts 2, but for their children and all those of future generations who would become Christians.

And, as we read on in Acts, we see this promise being fulfilled. The Spirit comes upon the Samaritans (Acts 8), on Paul (Acts 9), on the Roman centurion, Cornelius, and his household (Acts 10), and on the Ephesians (Acts 19). These all had similar experiences to the disciples on the day of Pentecost and nowhere does the New Testament suggest that they are not for today. Indeed, the experience of millions of Christians alive today confirms that it is!

But that does not mean that all have received it. In Acts the normal experience of those coming to faith in Christ was repentance followed immediately by baptism in water and baptism in the Spirit. Those who, like the Samaritans in Acts 8, did not receive the Spirit immediately after they were baptised in water, received soon after through the laying on of the apostles' hands (Acts 8:17, 19:6). Today, sadly, this is far less common, even among Christians who believe in these things. The root cause of this is, I believe, lack of teaching on the part of church leaders, an issue I will be addressing in the final chapter of this book.

So, to summarise, the baptism in the Spirit was promised by Jesus in Acts 1:5, was received by the first disciples when they were filled with the Spirit in Acts 2:4, was made available to all who would repent and be baptised (Acts 2:38), and received by subsequent disciples in Acts chapters 8, 9. 10, and 19. It's not the same as the Spirit's work in salvation or sanctification, but is an enduement with power for service accompanied by miraculous manifestations including speaking in tongues.

Baptism in the Spirit as the gateway to the gifts

Now from all that we have seen from the book of Acts, it must surely be clear that the baptism in the Spirit is the gateway to supernatural gifts. In Acts the baptism in the Spirit always came *before* the manifestation of spiritual gifts. The first disciples did not begin to speak in tongues until they were first filled with the Spirit at Pentecost (Acts 2:4).

The same is true of Cornelius and his household (Acts 10:44-46). And in Acts 19:1-6 the Ephesians spoke in tongues and prophesied after the Holy Spirit came upon them. Indeed, the fact that people were usually baptised in the Spirit on the day they were saved suggests that they could not possibly have received spiritual gifts before being baptised in the Spirit.

But can we *insist* that the baptism in the Spirit must come before the manifestation of spiritual gifts? After all, we read in the Gospels that Jesus' disciples worked miracles and this was, of course, before their baptism in the Spirit at Pentecost. However, as we examine these passages we discover that they did so in a special authority delegated to them by Jesus at that time. After Jesus went away, they needed the Spirit if they were to continue to work miracles (cf. John 14).

So from a biblical perspective the baptism in the Spirit is undoubtedly the gateway to spiritual gifts. But this raises the question of how it is that Christians who have a different understanding of what it means to be baptised in the Spirit can exercise spiritual gifts. How do we explain this?

Perhaps the first thing to say is that **we must decide what to believe on the basis of what we understand the Bible teaches, not on the basis of someone's experience**. Once we have done that, we may evaluate that experience in the light of Scripture, rather than trying to read our experience into God's word.

Personally, I distinguish between what I see in the Bible, and therefore teach, and what God in his grace may do today even if it is not completely in line with my understanding of the biblical pattern. God is far more willing to give than we are to receive. He is longing to lavish his gifts upon his people if only we would desire them more!

This means that he is pleased when any of his children seek after any spiritual gift, whether or not they have come to understand or believe in the baptism in the Holy Spirit.

This may well explain, for example, why some have been greatly used in healing even though they have a different understanding of what it means to be baptised in the Spirit. In my view we should thank God for the way he is using them, but still encourage them to receive the baptism in the Spirit with its accompanying blessing of speaking in tongues, for how else will they be able to pray with their spirit (1 Corinthians 14:14ff)?

But instead of looking at the experience of others we would do better to consider our own. If we have been baptised in the Spirit, we should press on to the gifts by eagerly desiring them and praying for them[15]. And if we have not yet received the baptism in the Spirit, we should ask God to fill us today. Our heavenly Father does give the Holy Spirit to those who ask him (Luke 11:13) and Jesus said that if we are thirsty we will drink (John 7:37-39). As we reach out in faith he will not disappoint us[16].

But it's now time to apply what we've learnt from Acts to what Paul says in 1 Corinthians 12:13.

---

[15] See *Body Builders,* Chapter 15.

[16] For practical help on how to receive the baptism in the Holy Spirit, see *The Holy Spirit – an Introduction*, Chapter 7.
See also *A New Dimension – How to be filled with the Holy Spirit*

How our understanding of Acts relates to 1 Corinthians 12:13

Perhaps the first thing to say is that, because the baptism in the Spirit was so vital to the experience of the early church, it's unthinkable that Paul could have a radically different understanding of what it means to be baptised in the Spirit from what we have discovered in Acts. So what we've learnt from Acts must inform our understanding of what he means in 1 Corinthians 12:13 when, following my translation, he says that we were *all baptised in the Spirit for the benefit of the one body.*

And we have seen from Acts that the baptism in the Spirit is a supernatural experience accompanied by speaking in tongues and leading to other charismatic gifts. We saw that it's not to be confused with conversion or sanctification, but a distinct experience which equips the Christian with supernatural power to be a witness for Christ.

So both in Acts and in 1 Corinthians 12, baptism in the Spirit is closely related to supernatural gifts. In Acts the emphasis is on evangelism, while in Corinthians it's on the edification of the church. Or to put it slightly differently, in Acts the gifts which result from the baptism in the Spirit enable those who are not yet believers to come to faith, while in Corinthians they edify those who are already believers and strengthen their faith.

So Acts and 1 Corinthians 12:13 are in perfect harmony with regard to the baptism in the Spirit. The difference in emphasis is easily understood in the light of the fact that in Acts Luke is primarily concerned with evangelism in the power of the Spirit, and in 1 Corinthians 12-14 Paul is concerned with pastoral issues relating to the use of spiritual gifts in the worship of the church. The baptism in the Spirit enables both. So, if we're to expect the supernatural in our meetings (14:26, 12:1-11 etc), we are totally dependent on the Holy Spirit, and since spiritual gifts are operated by individual Christians, it's vital that those who do so are baptised in the Holy Spirit.

To summarise, then, in 1 Corinthians 12:13 Paul is referring to the same experience as Luke describes in Acts, where Christians receive the power of the Spirit accompanied by the manifestation of supernatural gifts. Those gifts are vitally important, not only in confirming the message of the gospel, but also when Christians are gathered together in worship. It follows, therefore, that, if we are to see them in operation in our meetings as Paul teaches in 1 Corinthians 14:26, we need to encourage all Christians to be baptised in the Spirit. It is only through the power of the Spirit that we can properly fulfil our purpose as members of the body of Christ.

CHAPTER THREE

Everyone is needed

1 Corinthians 12:12-31

In the first chapter we saw from 1 Corinthians 14:26 that one of the features to be expected when Christians come together is the power of the Holy Spirit manifested in the use of supernatural gifts which are given as the Holy Spirit determines to individual Christians for the benefit of the church. In the last chapter we discussed the meaning and importance of the baptism in the Spirit as the gateway to those gifts.

In this chapter we'll be considering 1 Corinthians 12:12-31 and its bearing on those words in 14:26 where Paul says **every one of you has.** His clear intention is that they should all actively participate in the worship of the church, but they needed to do so in a spirit of unity and love. Their lack of love was evident from the serious divisions in the church (chapters 1-4), their need to consider others in the way they exercised their freedom (chapters 8-10), and their selfish behaviour at the Lord's Supper described in chapter 11.

In the light of all this, it's easy to understand why Paul felt the need to address the question of unity in chapter 12, of the importance of love in chapter 13, and of the need to put other people first in chapter 14. Keeping all this in mind will help us to understand more clearly the passage in 12:12-31. We also need to remember that in the first part of the chapter Paul has been dealing with supernatural gifts as this is the immediate context of the passage we are about to consider. In verse 12 Paul says:

> *For the body is a unit, though it is made up of many parts; and though all its parts are many, they form one body. So it is with Christ.*

The use of the word *for* shows that there is a link between what Paul has just said in verse 11 with what he's about to say in verse 12, and this indicates that supernatural gifts are still very much in mind. However, the subject is now broader, and Paul's teaching applies, not just to supernatural gifts, but to every function of the body, by which Paul clearly means the church, the body of Christ. He is drawing a parallel between the church and the human body. Just as each human being has one body which is made up of many parts, so too the church, which is the body of Christ, is one body with many parts.

Paul goes on to develop this theme in the following verses where the major themes are **unity** and **interdependence** in the midst of **diversity**[17]. He shows that all the members of the body are different (diversity) but are united by the fact that they are all part of the *same* body and empowered by the *same* Spirit (unity). Each part of the body is dependent on each of the other parts. Everyone is needed (interdependence). Just as the parts of the human body all need each other, so the individual members of the church all need each other.

---

[17] The list below outlines the verse references for each of these themes:

    Diversity: 4, 5, 6, 8-11, 12, 14, 20, 28.

    Unity: One Spirit: 4, 5, 6, 8, 9, 11, 13.

                  One Body: 12, 13, 20, 24-25.

    Interdependence: 21, 25, 26.

We will now consider this in more detail under the following headings:

- The illustration of the human body (14-26)
- The illustration applied to the church (27-31).

The illustration of the human body (14-26)

Paul's use of the human body as an illustration of the church and its members is easy enough for even a child to understand. He reminds us that our body *is not made up of one part but of many* (14). He then mentions different parts of the body – feet, hands, ears, and eyes – to point out that **every part of the body is needed**. Just because a foot is not a hand, it does not mean that it's not part of the body (15) and just because an ear is not an eye, it does not mean that it's not part of the body (16). In fact,

> *If the whole body were an eye, where would the sense of hearing be? If the whole body were an ear, where would the sense of smell be?* (17).

Paul then goes on to say that *God has arranged the parts in the body, every one of them, just as he wanted them to be* (18). And because it is **God** who has done so, it follows that every part is necessary. No part can say to another, *I don't need you* (20-21). Even the weaker and unpresentable parts are indispensable (22-23). And that's why there should be no division in the body. Its unity is expressed in all the parts having *equal concern for each other* (25) and the fact that,

> *If one part suffers, every part suffers with it; if one part is honoured, every part rejoices with it* (26).

Now it should be clear that in this passage Paul has been reminding the Corinthians of things they already know about their own physical bodies. But by telling them at the beginning (12) that the *church* is the body he is really concerned with, he knows that the Corinthians will have a pretty good idea of what he is getting at.

And so should we. The key lessons are as follows:

- The church is the body of Christ (12, 27)
- The parts (or members) of that body are individual Christians (27).
- Every member is different from all the others, but every member needs all the others (21).
- Every member is needed because God has put them just where he wants them to be (18, 24). Everyone is indispensable (22). Everyone is special (23).
- No member should ever say of themselves, *I am not a part of the body* (15-17). We mustn't think of ourselves as useless. Whether we believe it or not, like it or not, we belong to the body.
- No member should ever say of another member, *They are not a part of the body*. We mustn't think of anyone as useless (21-24).
- All the members should have equal concern for each other (25).

We'll consider *how* all this affects our understanding of 14:26 after we have examined verses 27-31.

The illustration applied to the church (27-31)

In verse 27 Paul says:

> *Now you are the body of Christ, and each one of you is a part of it.*

Paul now begins to apply to the church the principles he has been teaching in verses 12-26, and it's important at this stage to remind ourselves of something we have mentioned already. What Paul is saying is not only applicable to when we gather for worship – though that, of course, is our main focus in this book – but to the wider ministry of the church. The body of Christ is at work 24/7, not just for an hour or so on Sundays! This is reflected in verse 28, where Paul says:

> *And in the church God has appointed first of all apostles, second prophets, third teachers, then workers of miracles, also those having gifts of healing, those able to help others, those with gifts of administration, and those speaking in different kinds of tongues.*

Here Paul lists some of the different gifts and ministries that function within the body of Christ. These are not intended as an exhaustive list, but as representative samples of how different parts of the body are at work, whether in a church meeting or outside it.

It is not my intention to discuss in detail the precise nature of each of these gifts. I have already done so at length in *Body Builders* (where, incidentally, I suggest that the Greek translated by NIV as *those able to help others, those with gifts of administration,* might be better understood to refer to the roles of deacons and elders).

But what's important here is to notice that Paul begins by saying **God** *has appointed*. This re-emphasises what he has already said in verses 18 and 24:

> **God** *has arranged* (18) and **God** *has combined* (24).

We are what we are because that's what **God** has made us, and that's why every member of the body is important. Whether we are an Ephesians 4:11 gift, like apostle, prophet, or teacher, or whether we have supernatural gifts like working miracles, or healing, or speaking in tongues, we need to understand that it is by the grace of God that we are what we are and have what we have. As Paul later says of himself,

> *...by the grace of God I am what I am* (15:10).

Here Paul is referring to his role as a church leader, an apostle, and it's significant that, in the list we are now considering, he puts apostles first. And although it's unlikely that he's implying some form of hierarchy when he says, *first apostles, secondly prophets, thirdly teachers,* it's clear from chapter 14 (and especially 14:37) that Paul understood that the use of spiritual gifts like prophecy, tongues, and interpretation was subject to his apostolic authority.

Turning now to verses 29-30, we see that Paul repeats (in question form) the list of functions he has mentioned in verse 28 – though note the omission of *those able to help others*, and *those with gifts of administration,* which is probably because Paul felt it unnecessary to repeat all the functions listed in verse 28 to make his point. He says:

> *Are all apostles? Are all prophets? Are all teachers? Do all work miracles? Do all have gifts of healing? Do all speak in tongues? Do all interpret?*

The sense of these verses is very clear. The questions are rhetorical. The answer Paul clearly expects to each question is NO. Paul is reiterating his point that just as all the parts of our body are different and have different functions, so too all the members of the church are different and have different roles to play in the body of Christ.

It's particularly important to understand this when we consider the implication of his question, *Do all speak in tongues?* which clearly indicates that all do not. This is sometimes used as an argument against the teaching that we should expect to speak in tongues when we are baptised in the Holy Spirit[18], but that argument is easily dismissed when we bear in mind the context of Paul's question which, as we have seen, relates to functions within the *church*.

This is confirmed by his next question, *Do all interpret?* The purpose of the gift of interpretation of tongues is the edification of the *church* (14:5) and it is clear, therefore, that when Paul says *Do all speak in tongues?* he is referring to the use of tongues in church. However, in chapter 14 Paul distinguishes between the use of tongues in church and its use in private:

> *I thank God that I speak in tongues more than all of you. But in the church I would rather speak five intelligible words to instruct others than ten thousand words in a tongue* (18-19).

This surely indicates that in private Paul valued highly his ability to speak in tongues. This is how he could pray with his spirit (14:14-15) and was a valuable way of edifying himself spiritually (14:4), but in church his teaching gift would be of more benefit to other members of the body of Christ.

---

[18] See Chapter 2

Once we have understood the clear distinction Paul makes between the use of tongues in church and its use in private, the meaning of his question in 12:30 becomes very clear.

> *Does everybody speak in tongues with a view to its being interpreted for the edification of the church? No.*

That does not mean, however, that it would not be beneficial for every Christian to speak in tongues privately in order to *pray with their spirit.* And that ability, as we have seen from Acts, was imparted when new converts were baptised in the Holy Spirit.

But we must now turn our attention to how Paul's teaching in 1 Corinthians 12 affects our understanding of 14:26, where he says:

> *What then shall we say, brothers and sisters? When you come together, everyone has a hymn, or a word of instruction, a revelation, a tongue or an interpretation. All of these must be done for the strengthening of the church.*

1 Corinthians 14:26 in the light of chapter 12

In the Introduction to this book we identified three key principles in this verse – **participation, variety, and edification**. These principles may be seen as a summary of all that Paul is teaching in these chapters and all three are implicit in his teaching in chapter 12. In fact, what Paul says in chapter 12 enriches our understanding of what he means in 14:26.

With regard to **participation**, in 14:26 Paul says, *When you come together, **everyone has...*** or as later versions of NIV put it, ***each of you has.*** The implication is that every member of the body has the potential to bring something to the meeting that will be a blessing to others.

In chapter 12 we see examples of the kind of things that people might bring, and we're told that *in all of them **and in everyone** it is the same God at work* (6). The Spirit distributes his gifts ***to each one, just as he determines*** (11). And, as we have seen, the major emphasis of verses 12-26 is that every part of the body is needed. *The head cannot say to the hand, I don't need you* (21). So, if everyone is needed, there must surely be room for them to participate.

With regard to **variety,** in 14:26 Paul mentions *a hymn, or a word of instruction, a revelation, a tongue or an interpretation.* There are three main elements here – the musical, the doctrinal, and the supernatural. We will say more about these when we reach chapter 14, but it's evident that Paul expected all these elements to be present when Christians meet in church.

It's interesting that in chapter 12 Paul appears to say nothing about music, though it would undoubtedly be included in the *different kinds of service* he mentions in verse 5. He also says little in this chapter about doctrine, although its importance is strongly implied in verse 1 where he says that he does not want his readers *to be ignorant,* and he mentions *teachers* in verse 28. But we need have no doubt about Paul's view of the importance of sound doctrine, which is evidently his major purpose in writing his letters and becomes very evident in his teaching in chapter 15 on the most important doctrine of all – the resurrection of Christ.

However, if in chapter 12 he has nothing to say directly about music, and relatively little to say about doctrine, he has plenty to say about the supernatural. We have already seen that the gifts he lists in verses 8-10 are supernatural gifts, that the supernatural is still in mind in his illustration of the human body as the body of Christ, the church, and that supernatural gifts are still very much in evidence towards the end of the chapter in verses 28 and 29. It seems likely, therefore, that the variety he has in mind in 14:26 would be far wider than the things he mentions there, and could well include any or all of the gifts and ministries he has talked about in chapter 12.

That brings us finally to the principle of **edification** of which Paul speaks in 14:26 when he says that a*ll of these must be done for the strengthening (or edification) of the church.* We will say much more about this when we come to chapter 14, where edification is the dominant theme of the chapter. For now it's sufficient to note that it also underlies his teaching in chapter 12. The gifts of the Spirit are distributed for the good of all (7). We are baptised in the Spirit for the benefit of the church (13). And each part of the body has been placed there by God for the benefit of all the members because we all need each other (14-26).

So chapter 12 enhances our understanding of what Paul teaches in 14:26, but it also sets the context for our understanding of what he about to say about love in 1 Corinthians 13. But that's our subject in the next chapter.

CHAPTER FOUR

We're Nothing without Love

1 Corinthians 13:1-13

1 Corinthians 13 is one of the best-known chapters in the Bible. It is often chosen as a reading at weddings and is widely recognised as one of the greatest statements that has ever been written on the nature of love. I well remember how it was read on the first and last day of every term in the Chapel at Brentwood School where I attended as a pupil in the 1950s.

Verses 4-8 are a favourite source of sermon material for many a preacher and Christians have often been challenged to replace the word *love* with their own name and ask how true these verses are in their own lives. By contrast, of course, all Paul says about love is wonderfully true as we look at the life of the Lord Jesus, and I confess I find it easier to use his name, rather than mine, to replace *love* throughout these verses:

> *4 Jesus is patient, Jesus is kind...*

So there can be no doubt that the truths Paul teaches about love in this chapter extend far beyond the context in which it is set. But they do nevertheless have an immediate relevance to all he is saying throughout chapters 11-14 about what should happen when Christians meet to worship the Lord.

And that is what we will be considering in this chapter. How does 1 Corinthians 13 affect our understanding of chapter 14, and of 14:26 in particular?

We will divide the chapter into three sections:

- It's all meaningless without love (1-3)
- The nature of love (4-8)
- Recognising our limitations (8-12)

It's all meaningless without love (1-3)

In the opening verses of the chapter Paul says:

> *1 If I speak in the tongues of men and of angels, but have not love, I am only a resounding gong or a clanging cymbal. 2 If I have the gift of prophecy and can fathom all mysteries and all knowledge, and if I have a faith that can move mountains, but have not love, I am nothing. 3 If I give all I possess to the poor and surrender my body to the flames, but have not love, I gain nothing.*

The general sense of this passage is very clear and requires little comment here[19]. In saying this, however, we must be careful not to diminish its importance. Its clarity must not detract from its urgency. Nothing is more important than love. Whatever gifts we may have and whatever we may do, if our motive is not love, it counts for nothing. Without love *I am nothing* (2) and *I gain nothing* (3).

---

[19] In *Body Builders* I have already discussed what Paul means with regard to controversial issues like the meaning of *tongues of angels* and whether martyrdom is a gift of the Spirit. I see no need to repeat my arguments here, as these things are not, in my view, directly relevant to the subject of this book.

This principle applies to every function of the body of Christ, not just to the things mentioned in these verses, which are just illustrations of it. As we saw in the last chapter, every part of the body is needed. Every member is important. And when one member suffers, we all suffer (12:26). Each member should have equal concern for every other (12:25). And now in chapter 13 Paul says that the only way that all this is possible is when we love one another.

So the things Paul refers to in verses 1-3 are just illustrations of the great principle of the paramount importance of love. But why does he choose these *particular* illustrations to make his point? The answer must surely lie in the *particular* problems facing the church in Corinth at the time. It's evident from chapter 14 that there were problems in Corinth with their use of gifts like speaking in tongues and prophecy which are the two gifts he mentions first here in chapter 13. And the reference to knowledge may well reflect what Paul has said in chapter 8 about food sacrificed to idols, where he stresses the importance of love compared with knowledge:

> *We know that we all possess knowledge.* ***Knowledge puffs up, but love builds up.*** *The man who thinks he knows something does not yet know as he ought to know. But the man who loves God is known by God* (1-3).

This, along with the final verses of chapter 1, indicates that some of the Corinthians were in danger of boasting about their knowledge and wisdom. There Paul reminds them that they would be nothing if it were not for the fact that God had chosen them and called them:

> *Brothers,* ***think of what you were*** *when you were* ***called****. Not many of you were wise by human standards; not many were influential; not many were of noble birth.*

> But **God chose** the foolish things of the world to shame the wise; **God chose** the weak things of the world to shame the strong.
>
> He **chose** the lowly things of this world and the despised things – and the things that are not – to nullify the things that are, so that **no one may boast** before him.
>
> It is **because of him** that you are in Christ Jesus, who has become for us wisdom from God – that is, our righteousness, holiness and redemption. Therefore, as it is written: "**Let him who boasts boast in the Lord**" (1:26-31).

This is surely why he reminds them in 13:4 that *Love... does not boast.* And it may well account for the inclusion of *faith that can move mountains* (13:2). Spiritual gifts are *charismata.* They come from God's *grace.* There is no room for boasting, however greatly God may have used us.

So as we later consider Paul's encouragement in 14:26 for all to participate by bringing a contribution to our meetings, we need to remember that whatever we may bring must be brought in love and that, of course, includes humility. But now we need to consider how verses 4-8 might affect our understanding of 14:26.

The nature of love (4-8)
As I have already acknowledged, these verses have a far wider application than our understanding of chapter 14. But chapter 13 is no mere parenthesis. It is set firmly between Paul's teaching in chapter 12 on the importance of the role of every Christian within the church as the body of Christ and his application of that principle in chapter 14 where he gives specific direction as to how certain roles are to function when the church is gathered for worship.

Furthermore, the link in Paul's thinking between chapters 13 and 14 is clearly established in 14:1 where he says:

> *Follow the way of love and eagerly desire spiritual gifts, especially the gift of prophecy.*

As we will see in the next chapter, the underlying principle of all he says in chapter 14 is *putting other people first* which is surely the main way in which we express our love for them. Prophecy, for example, is to be desired more than tongues because it edifies others, not just ourselves (14:1-5). So his teaching on the nature of love in 13:4-8 has a direct application to our understanding of chapter 14 and of 14:26 in particular. But how? Paul says:

> *4 Love is patient, love is kind. It does not envy, it does not boast, it is not proud. 5 It is not rude, it is not self-seeking, it is not easily angered, it keeps no record of wrongs. 6 Love does not delight in evil but rejoices with the truth. 7 It always protects, always trusts, always hopes, always perseveres. 8 Love never fails.*

Some of these wonderful attributes of love are more obviously applicable to the contents of chapter 14 than others. So it is these that we'll consider here, bearing in mind that they also have a wider relevance that's beyond the scope of our present discussion.

Love is patient

In a gathering where each member is encouraged to contribute something for the edification of the others (14:26), there is an evident need for patience. Waiting one's turn isn't always easy, especially when some people are praying or prophesying at great length. As a preacher I confess that I have often been somewhat lacking in patience when the musicians are prolonging the worship to a point where I am wondering if there will be enough time left for me say all that I believe God's given me to say. But then I do well to remember that the congregation may well need to be patient with me!

Love is kind... it is not rude

Consideration for others is so important if the meeting is to meet its full potential. My old pastor, Alfred Webb, used to compare the time available in a meeting to a cake. If there were six people around the table, hopefully you wouldn't dream of taking more than one sixth of the cake! So, he said, don't take more than a fair share of the time available. Be kind. Making way for others is certainly taught in 14:30 where Paul encourages someone who is prophesying to stop if someone else has a revelation to share.

Of course, kindness in a meeting can take many forms, but perhaps one of the most important is with regard to judging other people's contributions to the meeting. Paul encourages us to *try to excel* in the use of the gifts God has given us (14:12), but that implies that the level at which we use them may not always be at the highest, and we are in need of kindness when this is clearly the case with regard to the contributions of others.

Love does not boast...It is not proud... It does not envy

We have already noted that pride was a major problem at Corinth – pride in who their favourite preacher was (chapter 1), pride in their tolerance (chapter 5), pride in their knowledge (chapter 8), and possibly, here in chapter 13, pride that they were able, so they believed, to speak the languages of angels (v1). There is also a suggestion of pride in 14:37 where Paul says:

> *If anybody thinks he is a prophet or spiritually gifted, let him acknowledge that what I am writing to you is the Lord's command.*

No doubt it would have been difficult for some to submit to Paul's apostolic authority in this matter, but the key to humility is the understanding that we are what we are by God's grace (15:10). Pride and boasting are totally inappropriate for a Christian:

> *For it is by grace you have been saved, through faith – and this not from yourselves, it is the gift of God – not by works, so that no one can boast. For we are God's workmanship, created in Christ Jesus to do good works, which God prepared in advance for us to do* (Ephesians 2:8-10).

All that we have and all that we are is by the grace of God. And this includes the gifts that we may use in our meetings. They are *charismata*. They come from God's grace. So there's no basis for pride, and there should really be no need for us to envy our fellow Christians, but sadly it's all too possible to do so.

We may envy the gifts God has given them, or the amount of time allotted to them, or the prominence given to them in the meeting. But if we love them we will be glad for them. Why am I glad when my children and grandchildren are taking part in the meetings? Because I love them! But as a Christian I am called to love *every* member of the body of Christ, and I should rejoice with them (12:26) when they are honoured.

Love is not self-seeking

That this was a problem in Corinth is clear from the fact that at the Lord's supper – which at that time would have been a meal rather than the tiny emblems that are generally used today – some were going hungry while others were getting drunk:

> *For as you eat, each of you goes ahead without waiting for anybody else. One remains hungry, another gets drunk* (11:21).

It's not surprising, therefore, that this self-centred attitude manifested itself in other areas too, as we see in the opening verses of chapter 14. The Corinthians were edifying *themselves* by speaking in tongues (v.4) but needed to be encouraged to prophesy so that others might be edified. But this is something we will address in more detail in the next chapter.

Love… rejoices with the truth… It always protects

Much of what Paul writes in his epistles is there for the express purpose of safeguarding the truth. What we believe is of vital importance. It determines our eternal destiny. And nowhere is this more important than when we are gathered together in church. Among the things that Paul encourages in 14:26 is *a word of instruction* – literally *a teaching.*

Love is to be the motive for all that we do, and that includes teaching. In Mark 6:34 we read that Jesus was moved with *compassion* for the people because they were like sheep without a shepherd, and so he began to *teach* them many things. In John 8:31-32 he said:

> *If you hold to my teaching, you are really my disciples. Then you will know the truth and the truth will set you free.*

Love was the motive for his teaching and its purpose was to set people free. The same must be true of those who bring a word of instruction in our meetings.

But the need for truth is relevant not only to teaching, but also to prophecy. As we shall see in the next section, *we know in part and we prophesy in part* (13:9). Our knowledge and prophetic insight are limited. That's why we all have a responsibility to *weigh carefully what is said* (14:29).

Recognising our limitations (8-12)

> *Love never fails, but where there are prophecies, they will cease; where there are tongues, they will be stilled; where there is knowledge, it will pass away. 9 For we know in part and we prophesy in part, 10 but when perfection comes, the imperfect disappears. 11 When I was a child, I talked like a child, I thought like a child, I reasoned like a child. When I became a man, I put childish ways behind me. 12 Now we see but a poor reflection as in a mirror; then we shall see face to face. Now I know in part; then I shall know fully, even as I am fully known. 13 And now these three remain: faith, hope and love. But the greatest of these is love.*

The overall sense of these verses is very clear. Paul has already taught us that supernatural gifts are pointless unless they are motivated by love (1-3). He has explained what he means by love and extolled its virtues (4-8). Now in verses 8-13 he makes it clear that, although there will ultimately be no need for supernatural gifts, love will remain for ever. It never fails (8). It remains (13).

In Chapter One we discussed what Paul means by *perfection* in verse 10. We rejected the views of the cessationists who believe that *perfection* refers to the completion of the canon of Scripture. The supernatural gifts of the Holy Spirit will be at work in the church right up until the Lord's return. In the age to come, prophecy will not be needed – it will have already been fulfilled! Words of knowledge will be unnecessary – we shall know fully, even as we are known! But until then, these wonderful gifts are essential to the effective witness and worship of the church.

But wonderful though these gifts are, their operation is not infallible. *We know **in part** and we prophesy **in part**.* The contributions Paul is encouraging in 14:26 must be understood in this light. God's gifts are perfect, but we are not. We do not yet see *face to face.* Paul says, ***we** know… **we** prophesy.* The gifts come from God but they come through **us**, and we are fallible.

This must affect our understanding of all that Paul says in chapter 14, not just verse 26. As we *eagerly desire* spiritual gifts we are to *try to excel* in our use of them (12). This clearly implies that it's possible to exercise them without excelling in them. That's why words of prophecy need to be *weighed carefully* (29) and why Paul found it necessary to give instruction as to how the gifts should be used. Had the operation of the gifts been infallible, such instruction would have been unnecessary.

In short, whatever contribution we may make during the course of a meeting, we must always be aware of our own fallibility. Paul encourages us to participate (26), but to make sure that we do so in love. Our use of spiritual gifts may well be imperfect, but he tells us to eagerly desire them (14:1) nevertheless. And that's something we will consider in more detail in the next chapter.

CHAPTER FIVE

Paul's Teaching on Tongues

in 1 Corinthians 14

So far in this book we have suggested that 1 Corinthians 14:26 should be taken as a serious indication of what God desires when we meet for worship, and we have been looking at chapters 12 and 13 to see how they might influence our understanding of this verse.

In chapter 13 Paul has demonstrated the futility of spiritual gifts unless they are exercised in love. He now goes on to give practical instructions concerning the use of the gifts in public worship. The underlying theme of the chapter is edification, which must be the basic motive for the exercise of spiritual gifts. Prophecy is seen as the most appropriate means of edifying both believers and unbelievers. The New Testament believers' meeting was a time when all should participate with a view to edifying the church (26).

In this chapter we'll be considering what Paul teaches in chapter 14 about speaking in tongues. In Chapters Six and Seven we'll consider what he says about interpretation of tongues and prophecy, as they are all mentioned in 14:26 and much of the rest of the chapter is taken up with these themes. As we do so, we will discover what Paul has to say about the value, purpose, and use of these gifts.

In Chapter Eight we'll be looking at some of the key principles which underlie his teaching, such as edification and the need for intelligibility, variety, order, and balance in our meetings. Handling things in this way will mean that we will not be moving through chapter 14 verse by verse, as Paul's teaching on tongues, for example, is scattered throughout the chapter.

In this chapter we will seek to answer three questions:

- How does Paul describe speaking in tongues?
- What is the purpose of speaking in tongues?
- How is speaking in tongues to be used in church?

How does Paul describe speaking in tongues?

Perhaps the first thing to say is that Paul uses the same Greek expression as is used by Luke when he describes the events that took place at Pentecost. Acts 2:4, when literally translated, reads:

> *They were all filled with the Holy Spirit and began to speak in different languages...*

I have translated the word for *tongues* here as *languages* for two reasons. First, because the context clearly shows that the disciples were speaking the languages of the people in the crowd, and secondly, because *tongues* is in fact just another rather old-fashioned word for *languages.* Our English word *language* is derived from the French word *langue* which can mean either *tongue* (the thing in your mouth you speak with) or *language* (the thing you speak).

The words used by both Luke and Paul are *laleo* (speak) and *glossa* (tongue or language). So when Paul talks about speaking in tongues he is referring to the same phenomenon as took place at Pentecost when the disciples spoke languages they had never learned. However, at Pentecost there were people present who recognised the languages the disciples were speaking, whereas usually there is no one present who will recognise the language we are speaking. This is probably why in 1 Corinthians 14:2 Paul says:

> *For the person speaking in a tongue does not speak to men but to God, for no one understands him, but he is speaking mysteries with his spirit* (my translation).

Here Paul tells us that when we speak in tongues we are speaking to God. This is because, unless it's interpreted, as we shall see later, no one can understand us. We are speaking mysteries with our spirit. Indeed, we ourselves do not understand what we are saying. This is confirmed in verse 14 where Paul says:

> *...if I pray in a tongue, my spirit prays, but my mind is unfruitful.*

So speaking in tongues is speaking a language we do not understand and which no one else can understand (unless, of course, we happen to be speaking their own language as the disciples did at Pentecost). When we speak in English we are speaking with our mind. We understand what we are saying. But when we speak in tongues we are speaking with our spirit, and we do not understand what we are saying.

In verse 14 Paul has described speaking in tongues as *praying* with our spirit, but in verse 16 it's clear that it can also be *praising*:

> *If you are **praising** God **with your spirit**, how can one who finds himself among those who do not understand say "Amen" to your **thanksgiving**, since he does not know what you are saying?*

So he also refers to it as *thanksgiving,* and this is repeated in verse 17 when he says*:*

> *You may be **giving thanks** well enough, but the other person is not edified.*

This is in harmony with what we read in Acts 2:11 when the bewildered crowd at Pentecost exclaimed:

> *We hear them **declaring the wonders of God** in our own tongues!*

This could either mean that the disciples were *praising* God in tongues or that they were *proclaiming the gospel*. The Greek word *musterion* which Paul uses in verse 2, which tells us that when we speak in tongues we are speaking *mysteries,* is used elsewhere in Paul's writings to refer to the gospel as a secret made known by God *to man* (my italics) through his Spirit (e.g. Ephesians 3:4-5).

So Paul describes speaking in tongues as speaking with our spirit rather than with our mind. He uses verbs like *speaking (2), praying (14), praising (16),* and *giving thanks (17)*. And, as at Pentecost, it can also be *a sign for unbelievers (22)*. But this is something we will discuss in the next section.

What is the purpose of speaking in tongues?

The apostle Paul valued very highly his ability to speak in tongues. In verse 18 he says:

> *I thank God that I speak in tongues more than all of you.*

But in verse 19 he adds:

> *But in the church I would rather speak five intelligible words to instruct others than ten thousand words in a tongue.*

This makes clear that, although he spoke in tongues a great deal when he was not in church – that is, when he was in private – he did not do so in public. In Chapter Three we have already shown how the distinction between the public and private use of tongues explains what Paul means when he says in 12:30, *Do all speak in tongues?* All may speak in tongues privately, but not all will do so publicly.

But chapter 14 sheds light on both these uses. The purpose of private tongues is, as we have already seen, that we might speak with our spirit as distinct from speaking with our mind. This may take the form of prayer, or praise, or thanksgiving. Used in this way it is an important means of building ourselves up spiritually, as Paul says in verse 4:

> *He who speaks in a tongue edifies himself.*

This is presumably why Paul valued so highly his personal use of tongues, and it may well be what he was referring to when he told Timothy to *fan into flame the gift of God* that he had received when Paul had laid his hands on him (2 Timothy 1:6-7). Verses 14-15 reveal Paul's personal determination to do the same:

> *For if I pray in a tongue, my spirit prays, but my mind is unfruitful. 15 So what shall I do? I **will** pray with my spirit, but I **will** also pray with my mind; I **will** sing with my spirit, but I **will** also sing with my mind.*

He is clearly recommending that we should do the same. And if we really want the Holy Spirit to move powerfully in our meetings, we will be willing to make time in private to pray, not only in English with our mind, but also in tongues with our spirit.

Now with regard to the purpose of the public use of tongues, we have already mentioned the day of Pentecost, where the miracle of unlearned Galileans speaking languages they had never learned led to the conversion of some 3000 people. But his was clearly not the scenario Paul had in mind when he said to the Corinthians that *tongues are a sign for unbelievers* (14:22).

It's clear from the next verse that, far from expecting unbelievers to come to faith when hearing speaking in tongues, he thinks it more likely that they will conclude that the Corinthians are out of their mind! So in what sense are tongues intended as a sign to those who do not believe? As we examine the passage in which he says this we find what at first sight appear to be two contradictions, one with regard to speaking in tongues and the other regarding prophecy:

- Regarding tongues, in verse 22 Paul says that they are a sign for unbelievers, but in verse 23 he implies that it's not good to speak in tongues in their presence in case they think you're out of your mind.

- Regarding prophecy, in verse 22 he says that it's not for unbelievers, but for believers. However, in verses 24 and 25 he says that if unbelievers come into a meeting where everyone is prophesying, they will be convinced that they are sinners and fall down and worship God.

So how do we explain these apparent contradictions? Paul's instructions are fairly clear. He is continuing the theme he started at the beginning of the chapter that prophecy is preferable to tongues because it's more helpful to believers. And now, he says, it is more helpful to unbelievers too. So if unbelievers come in, it's better to prophesy than to speak in tongues.

But the argument he uses to back up this teaching is extremely difficult to follow. However, one possible way of resolving the difficulty is to begin by taking the reference to prophecy in verse 22 as referring, not to the gift of prophecy, but to the prophecy of from Isaiah 28:11-12 that he has just quoted[20]. Taken this way, verses 21-24 could be paraphrased as follows:

> 21 In the law it has been written that I will speak to this people in other tongues (even though they are an *unbelieving* people, as the context of Isaiah 28:11 makes clear) and yet *they will not listen* to me, says the Lord (Isaiah 28:12).
>
> 22 So, on the basis of the quote from Isaiah, tongues were and are given as a sign to unbelieving people. However, **the** prophecy (Isaiah 28:11-12) is not given for the benefit of the unbelievers but for us believers in order that we might act upon it in the following way:
>
> 23 (Because Isaiah's prophecy was written for us believers telling us that unbelievers would not hear even the sign of tongues), when we gather together in worship we shouldn't speak in tongues when unbelievers are present, because it's a sign they will reject (and will only lead to their condemnation – just as the unknown languages of Israel's foreign invaders in Isaiah served as a sign of God's pending judgment).

---

[20] Abstract nouns like *prophecy* usually take the definite article in Greek, whereas in English we leave it out. So *he propheteia* can be either translated *prophecy* or **the** *prophecy*. In Matthew 13:14-15, for example, *he propheteia* is used to refer to a specific quotation from the prophecy of Isaiah. It is possible that Paul is doing the same here.

> 24 On the other hand, if we all prophesy the unbeliever will be convinced...

Although we cannot be sure that I am right in understanding the passage in this way, this suggestion does overcome a notorious difficulty for which, in my view, no satisfactory explanation has been offered so far. But, even if it's correct, we still have the difficulty that Paul's warning that, if we all speak in tongues unbelievers will say that we are out of our mind, appears to be contradicted by events on the day of Pentecost.

However, we need to remember that in Acts 2, when some 3000 people were added to the church, the first effects of the miracle of tongues were bewilderment (6), amazement and perplexity (12), and, on the part of some, cynicism (13). It was the preaching of the gospel by Peter that led to their conversion. So Paul's warning that speaking in tongues may lead to opposition, and his insistence that prophecy – speaking words that people can understand – is preferable to tongues, are not out of harmony with Acts 2.

On the basis of all this, it's better, in my view, to consider the use of tongues as a sign to unbelievers as something exceptional[21]. We rarely, if ever, know that a language we may be speaking in tongues is going to be recognised by someone present and we must trust the Holy Spirit to enable us to speak that language if he so determines. He alone knows what impact it will have on the hearer.

---

[21] There are of course many documented cases of tongues being recognised as the language of someone listening. See footnote 6. See also two examples from my own ministry recorded in *Signs from Heaven – Why I believe*.

But this is by no means the only way that tongues may be used in public, as Paul makes clear in the opening verses of chapter 14, where he says:

> *Follow the way of love and eagerly desire spiritual gifts, especially the gift of prophecy.*
>
> *2 For anyone who speaks in a tongue does not speak to men but to God. Indeed, no one understands him; he utters mysteries with his spirit.*
>
> *3 But everyone who prophesies speaks to men for their strengthening, encouragement and comfort.*
>
> *4 He who speaks in a tongue edifies himself, but he who prophesies edifies the church.*
>
> *5 I would like every one of you to speak in tongues, but I would rather have you prophesy. He who prophesies is greater than one who speaks in tongues, unless he interprets,* **so that the church may be edified**.

The reference to interpretation of tongues in verse 5 makes clear the purpose of its use. It's for the edification of the church. Tongues are unintelligible unless they are interpreted and without interpretation the speaker is just speaking *into the air* (9). But when interpreted they can fulfil a similar function to prophecy, which also edifies the church (4) bringing *strengthening, encouragement and comfort* (3).

We will return to this in the next chapter when we consider Paul's teaching on the gift of interpretation of tongues, but for now it's sufficient to note that the purpose of the use of tongues in church must surely be the same as that of the gift of interpretation – namely, the edification, strengthening, encouragement and comfort of believers.

How is speaking in tongues to be used in church?

Despite Paul's clear teaching that prophecy is preferable to tongues (1-5), he by no means discourages the use of tongues in church. Although in verse 5 he says that he would rather have them prophesy, he does say, nevertheless, *I would like every one of you to speak in tongues.* And we have already seen that he expects speaking in tongues to be a regular part of the worship of the church (26) and it is certainly not to be forbidden (39).

However, the key to its use in church is that it needs to be interpreted so that everyone may be edified. In fact, in verse 28 he tells us that

> *If there is no interpreter, the speaker should keep quiet in the church and speak to himself and God.*

This suggests that the personal use of tongues in church is not prohibited, but it must be done quietly as it will edify no one except the speaker (cf. 4). Speaking out loud in tongues, therefore, is to be strongly discouraged unless it is intended that it be interpreted, and that of course will require someone with the gift of interpretation to be present.

This may, of course, be the person who has spoken in tongues, as in verses 12-13 Paul encourages those who speak in tongues to pray for the gift of interpretation:

> *So it is with you. Since you are eager to have spiritual gifts, try to excel in gifts that build up the church.* 13 *For this reason*

> *anyone who speaks in a tongue should pray that he may interpret what he says.*

But if a person who wants to speak in tongues does not possess the gift of interpretation, they must first make sure that someone is present who does, and if not, they must speak quietly to themselves and to God (28).

However, if an interpreter is present, the speaker in tongues may speak out loud with a view to its being interpreted for the edification of the church, subject to the conditions Paul gives in verse 27, where he says:

> *If anyone speaks in a tongue, two, or at the most three, should speak, one at a time, and someone must interpret.*

This instruction is so clear that it hardly requires further comment, but we will discuss some of the practical implications in the next chapter.

Conclusion

In this chapter we have seen that when Paul uses the term *speaking in tongues,* he is referring to the same gift as the disciples received on the day of Pentecost – the ability to speak languages they had never learned. We saw that tongues may be expressed in a variety of ways, including, prayer, praise, thanksgiving, and declaring the wonders of God.

We discovered that when we speak in tongues it's our spirit that is praying, not our mind. God gives us this gift to help us edify ourselves – to build ourselves up spiritually. It is also given so that when it's interpreted it will edify the church. And it can be used as a sign to unbelievers when, as at Pentecost, they understand the language that is being spoken.

Finally, we saw that Paul does expect this gift to be in operation in our meetings, but that it should be used quietly if it is not for interpretation. It must only be spoken aloud if an interpreter is present, and it must be used only two, or at the most three, times in a meeting. We will consider this further in the next chapter when we examine Paul's teaching on the gift of interpretation.

CHAPTER SIX

Paul's Teaching on Interpretation of Tongues in 1 Corinthians 14

The gift of interpretation of tongues is a gift imparted by the Holy Spirit that enables Christians to understand what is said when someone speaks in tongues. It is given to individual Christians, as determined by the Holy Spirit, with the specific purpose of edifying the church.

Paul's entire teaching on this gift is found in 1 Corinthians, chapters 12 and 14. In chapter 12 it is mentioned twice, first in verse 10 where it is mentioned among the list of supernatural gifts given to individual Christians as the Holy Spirit determines, and then in verse 30 where Paul asks the rhetorical question, *Do all interpret?* clearly implying that all do not.

This means that apart from Paul's overall teaching on supernatural gifts, much of which we have outlined in Chapter One, our main source of material for understanding this gift is found in 1 Corinthians 14. In this chapter I will:

- Examine the references to interpretation of tongues.
- Discuss certain practical issues that arise from this.
- Share a personal testimony.

References to interpretation in 1 Corinthians 14

These are found in verses 5, 13, and 26-28. We will examine each of these in turn.

Verse 5

> *The person who prophesies is greater than the person who speaks in tongues, unless they interpret so that the church may be edified.*

This verse makes clear the purpose of the gift – the edification of the church. We have already seen that in verses 1-5 Paul is arguing that prophecy is preferable to tongues because prophecy edifies the church whereas speaking in tongues does not because no one can understand it (2).

Here, however, he acknowledges that if speaking in tongues is interpreted it can edify the church, in which case it is as valuable as prophecy. But this need not mean that it's necessarily the same as prophecy. We will discuss this later when we consider the form the gift should take.

Verse 13

In verse 12 Paul underlines his teaching that the main purpose of spiritual gifts is to build up the church by telling the Corinthians to *try to excel in gifts that build up the church.* This gives the reason for what he says in verse 13.

> *Anyone who speaks in a tongue should pray that they may interpret what they say.*

He says this because the only way that speaking in tongues will edify other Christians is if it is interpreted. This does not mean, however, that all interpretation should be given by the person who has spoken in tongues. Far from it. The interpretation may very well be given by someone else. And to allow someone other than the speaker in tongues to interpret means that more people are participating in the meeting, something Paul is keen to encourage, as the next passage makes clear.

Verses 26-28

> 26 *What then shall we say, brothers? When you come together, everyone has a hymn, or a word of instruction, a revelation, a tongue or an interpretation. All of these must be done for the strengthening of the church. 27 If anyone speaks in a tongue, two – or at the most three – should speak, one at a time, and someone must interpret. 28 If there is no interpreter, the speaker should keep quiet in the church and speak to himself and God.*

Verse 26 is the key verse upon which this book is based. It gives clear guidance on the sort of things we should expect in our meetings, and it's noteworthy that tongues and interpretation are included in what Paul is recommending. But note the use of the word *if* in verse 27:

> *If anyone speaks in a tongue…*

This shows us that Paul does not automatically assume that there will be speaking in tongues in the meeting. The things mentioned in verse 26 are not obligatory ingredients for every meeting. They are the kind of things to expect, but not necessarily in every meeting. The manifestation of spiritual gifts will vary from meeting to meeting as the Spirit leads. The main point is that whatever is taking place, everything *must be done for the strengthening of the church.*

So, *if anyone speaks in tongues,* what should happen next? Paul is quite clear on this as the following literal translation shows:

> *If anyone speaks in a tongue, let it be by two or at the most three people. And let one person interpret* (my translation).

At first sight the first part of the verse is reasonably clear. Paul seems to be saying that during the course of a meeting, no more than three people should speak in tongues. But this clearly applies to the use of tongues for the purpose of interpretation, because he says, *Let one person interpret.* However, he does allow for the private use of tongues in church, provided that this is done quietly, speaking to oneself and to God (28) and this need not be limited to three people because it is done privately.

Furthermore, even with regard to the use of tongues for interpretation, bearing in mind the flexibility of starting and finishing times that would have been current in Corinth, it's possible that Paul meant no more than two or three people should speak in tongues before moving on to other things. We will consider this further when we discuss practical issues that arise from Paul's teaching.

Another practical issue that we will need to consider in due course is how to understand and apply the final part of verse 27, which NIV translates as, *Someone must interpret,* but which KJV translates this as,

> *Let **one** interpret* (my emphasis),

which is the literal translation of the Greek word that Paul uses here. The word is *heis* and students of Greek will know that this is used for the numeral 1. (The Greek for 1, 2, 3, is *heis, duo, treis*). It occurs 20 times in 1 Corinthians and everywhere else it can only mean *one*. That's why, in the translation I offered earlier I translated it as

> *Let one person interpret.*

But does this mean that Paul is saying that if there are two or three utterances in tongues, the same person should give the interpretation for all of them, as some have suggested? I think not, and I will give my reasons for saying so later.

Finally, we have already commented on verse 28 in the last chapter with regard to speaking in tongues, but Paul's use of the word *interpreter* is interesting. He says:

> *If there is no interpreter, the speaker (in tongues) should keep quiet in the church and speak to himself and God.*

The term *interpreter* clearly indicates that those who exercised the gift of interpretation were seen as permanently possessing the gift. If that were not so, how could the speaker in tongues know whether there was an interpreter present or not? Supernatural gifts are not something which God gives and then takes away. They are **given** to individual Christians (12:8-11) for the benefit of the church. A person who has interpreted once can be expected to do so again. Obviously this places a heavy responsibility on the interpreter, as I know from my own experience, which I will share in the last part of the chapter.

Practical issues arising from Paul's teaching

The form the gift should take

We saw in the last chapter that Paul describes speaking in tongues as *speaking with our spirit* as distinct from *speaking with our mind* (14:14). This may take any one of several different forms – prayer, praise, thanksgiving, and speaking *mysteries*, which, we said, could well be connected with declaring the wonders of God revealed in the truths of the gospel. Now, if the gift of interpretation enables us to understand what is being said when someone speaks in tongues, it follows that the interpretation should take the same form as the tongue, whether prayer, or praise, or thanksgiving etc.

It's my view that interpretation can take any of these forms and it would be wrong to limit its expression to just one of them. However, in some churches interpretation almost always takes the form of a prophecy and in others it tends to take the form of praise. Those who take the view that interpretation should take the form of a prophecy base their argument on 14:5 where Paul says:

> *The person who prophesies is greater than the person who speaks in tongues, unless they interpret so that the church may be edified.*

The argument goes like this. Prophecy edifies the church. Interpretation edifies the church. Therefore, the interpretation of tongues equals prophecy. But there is a logical flaw in this argument. It's like saying,

> *Tea is a drink. Coffee is a drink.*
>
> *Therefore, tea is the same as coffee!*

Paul says that both prophecy and interpretation edify the church, but that does not necessarily mean that they do so in the same way. If, for example, interpretation were to take the form of praise, rather than prophecy, would it not edify the church? And who is not edified by the psalms of praise? I have personally been greatly edified by both forms of interpretation.

Those who insist on praise interpretations base their argument on the NIV translation of 14:2, which reads:

> *For anyone who speaks in a tongue does not speak to men but to God. Indeed, no one understands him…*

So, it is argued, if the tongue is *to God*, the interpretation must be *to God*, in the form of either praise or prayer. However, as I explained in the last chapter, a more literal translation would be:

> *For the person speaking in a tongue does not speak to men but to God,* **for** *no one understands him, but he is speaking mysteries with his spirit* (my translation).

This makes clear that the reason for saying that speaking in tongues is *to God* is that no one can understand it. When the disciples spoke in tongues at Pentecost, did it not speak to men? And why was this? Because they understood what was being said. It follows, therefore, that if tongues in church can be understood through the use of the gift of interpretation, it can most certainly speak to us.

I have said more on this in the chapter on interpretation of tongues in *Body Builders*, but I hope that I have said enough here to show that both praise and prophecy style interpretations are legitimate manifestations of the gift and we should accept and encourage both.

Two or at the most three…

I suggested earlier that, bearing in mind the flexibility of starting and finishing times that would have been current in Corinth, Paul may have meant that no more than two or three people should speak in tongues before moving on to other aspects of worship. However, I am not convinced that this would be helpful for most of our meetings today, but during protracted meetings like days or nights of prayer it would make room for further expressions of the gift. For meetings of normal length, it would, in my view, be wise to apply quite strictly the limitations Paul imposes in this verse. But that raises the question, *What should we do if someone brings a fourth utterance in tongues? Should it be interpreted?*

The first thing to say in response to this is that it's unlikely to happen if the church has been taught how spiritual gifts should be operated in our meetings. However, on the rare occasion when it might happen, my own view is that it *should* be interpreted on the grounds that the overriding principle in Paul's teaching in this chapter is edification, and interpreted tongues are more edifying than tongues that are not interpreted.

However, to avoid repetition of this, I would gently point out to the congregation that the scriptural limit is two, or *at the most* three. But this is something about which the leaders of the church should decide in advance their interpretation of Paul's teaching and how it should be applied locally.

Let one person interpret

I said earlier that the Greek in verse 27 is best translated as, *Let **one** person interpret.* This in fact reflects how the Authorised Version translates it and, as a result of this, some churches have taught that, if there are two or three utterances in tongues, the same person should give the interpretation for all of them.

However, although this is a valid application of what Paul is saying, I think it more likely that his intention is to say that **each utterance in tongues needs only one person to interpret it** – an instruction that may well have been needful for the unruly members of the Corinthian church.

A personal testimony

I said earlier, when talking about Paul's use of the word *interpreter* (28), that a person who has interpreted once can be expected to do so again. Paul's teaching implies that, if we want to speak in tongues publicly, we need to check that there's an interpreter present. And if there is, we are free to go ahead. That places a heavy responsibility on the interpreter to be ready to interpret at any time, because we do not know when someone is going to speak in tongues..

I confess that I have sometimes found this difficult and am often tempted to doubt, wondering how I can be sure that any interpretation I might bring will be correct. But I have also discovered that, as we overcome our doubts by trusting the Lord, he does not let us down, as the testimony I'm about to share confirms.

I first started interpreting tongues as a student at Oxford, shortly after I was baptised in the Holy Spirit. The Pentecostal church I was attending in Oxford was a good church and the gifts of the Spirit were in evidence during most Sunday morning services. However, there were one or two occasions when speaking in tongues was not interpreted, and I was quite concerned because I knew that this was not in line with Scripture.

I shared my concern with a friend who was an evangelist and he said that the solution was simple. **I** should interpret it. But the problem was that I didn't have the gift of interpretation. To which he replied, *Then **ask** for it.* As I knew that this was in line with 1 Corinthians 14:13, I began to pray that God would give me the gift, and a few weeks later the opportunity came. Someone spoke in tongues, and I was expecting, and hoping, that someone else would interpret it! But when no one else did so, I began to speak out in faith, believing that

God would not let me down, yet wondering all the time if I was saying the right thing!

For months I wondered if the gift I had received was genuine, or whether it was 'just me'. Then, one day, at the close of a meeting in which I had interpreted, someone came up to me and told me that they had received word for word the interpretation which I had given. I had exercised the gift in faith for months, but finally I had God's confirmation that it was real. Similar confirmation has come dozens of times since. The following testimony is the most outstanding example.

In November 1977 I was serving as Acting Principal of Mattersey Hall Bible College prior to becoming Principal in 1978. One Saturday evening we took a bus-load of about 45 students to Bethshan Tabernacle in Manchester. There were several hundred people in the meeting during which the students sang and testified, and I preached. As soon as I had finished preaching, a woman near to the back of the meeting began to speak in tongues. As I was still at the microphone, it seemed appropriate for me to interpret so that everyone present would hear and be edified. As usual I spoke out in faith what I felt the Lord had put on my heart. When I had finished, we sang a hymn and the pastor closed the meeting in prayer.

As soon as the meeting was over, one of our students, Guetawende Roamba from Burkina Faso rushed up to me. He was clearly very excited, and when I asked him what was the matter, he told me that the woman who had spoken in tongues had been speaking his native language. Now in Burkina Faso they speak French, and because I also speak French fairly fluently, I knew that she had not been speaking French. So I wondered what language it might be.

What language? I asked. *Moré*, he replied. Frankly, at that time I had never heard of it – and we found out later that the Irish lady who had spoken in tongues had never heard of it either! But I was excited that I had been present when speaking in tongues had been recognised as a real language.

At the same time I was not a little concerned because I was the one who had given the interpretation! I had been interpreting tongues since I was a student at Oxford in 1960, but it had always been (as it always must be) 'by faith'. I had simply trusted the promise of Jesus that God gives good gifts to those who ask him (Matthew 7:11). Of course, I had no need to fear, but it's easy to imagine how embarrassed I would have been if I had 'got it wrong' in the presence of one of my Bible College students!

I hardly dared ask the question, but I knew I had to.

And what about the interpretation, Gueta? Was it accurate?

Of course, you know the answer, because I wouldn't be telling this story if the interpretation had been wrong!

What an amazing thing! The Holy Spirit inspired an Irish woman to speak an African language which she had never heard, or even heard of, and then gave the interpretation to an English man who had never heard of it either! God is faithful. His word is true. And his Spirit is still at work distributing his gifts as he himself determines.

CHAPTER SEVEN

Paul's Teaching on Prophecy in 1 Corinthians 14

Having discussed Paul's teaching on tongues and interpretation in 1 Corinthians 14, we now turn to the subject of prophecy. We will consider what it is, its value and purpose, its limitations, and its use in church.

What is prophecy?

In both Old and New Testaments the basic meaning of the word *prophesy* is to *speak on behalf of someone else*. A good illustration of this can be found in Exodus 7: 1-2 where the Lord says to Moses:

> *See, I have made you like God to Pharaoh, and your brother Aaron will be your prophet. You are to say everything I command you, and your brother Aaron is to tell Pharaoh to let the Israelites go...*

Aaron is called Moses' prophet because he is going to speak on his behalf. Understood this way, to prophesy is to hear from God and then pass on to others what he has said[22].

Today, however, prophecy is often used to mean foretelling the future, but although it can contain an element of prediction, this is not its essential meaning. And it should not be confused with

---

[22] For a more detailed study of this, see the chapters on *Prophets* and *The Gift of Prophecy* in *Body Builders*.

preaching or teaching. In *Body Builders* I described the gift of prophecy as:

> speaking on behalf of God by the supernatural inspiration of the Holy Spirit for the strengthening, encouragement and comfort of the church. It may at times contain elements of revelation or even prediction, but must be distinguished from the ministry of the teacher whose message comes from God by way of the Scriptures.

In the New Testament, apart from the many references back to the prophecies contained in the Old Testament, we find that there are three different ways in which the words *prophecy* and *prophesy* are used.

First, remembering that the basic meaning of *prophesy* is to speak on behalf of someone, as God's people there's a sense in which we can all 'prophesy' because we are all called to speak on his behalf. The purpose of the Spirit's coming at Pentecost was that we might receive power to be witnesses (Acts 1:8). The Spirit was poured out so that all God's people could prophesy – sons and daughters, young and old, servants, men and women (Acts 2:16-18).

Secondly, however, although we are speaking for God when we witness for Jesus, it is not the same as the gift of prophecy that brings *strengthening, encouragement and comfort* to the church (14:3). In 12:8-11, where Paul lists nine spiritual gifts, one of which is prophecy, he says:

> *...to **another** prophecy... he (the Spirit) gives them to each person just as he determines.*

This shows that this gift is not given to everybody, and Romans 12:6 backs this up by saying:

> We have **different** gifts according to the grace given us. **If a man's gift is prophesying...**

So, although all Christians are to 'prophesy' in the general sense of speaking on God's behalf, not all will exercise the gift of prophecy Paul talks about in 1 Corinthians.

And, thirdly, not all who exercise the gift of prophecy will be prophets in the Ephesians 4:11 sense. In *Body Builders* I have suggested that the clearest role of a New Testament[23] prophet is to be seen in the ministry of Agabus who spoke with great revelation from the Spirit (Acts 11:27-28, 21:10). This included the accurate prediction of certain future events. His prophecy about a widespread famine (Acts 11:27-30) and his prediction of Paul's captivity in Jerusalem (Acts 21:11) are well-known examples of this. They demonstrate that his ministry involved more than the simple gift of prophecy. In short:

- All God's people should prophesy (speak on his behalf).
- Not all will receive the gift of prophecy (to edify the church).
- Not all of these will exercise the ministry of a prophet like Agabus.

---

[23] Old Testament prophets do not serve well as an illustration of the role of prophets today. Before Pentecost only a few people experienced the Spirit. Since Pentecost the gift of the Spirit has been available to all (Acts 2:17). It's the privilege of all God's children to be led by his Spirit (Romans 8:14). The role of prophets since Pentecost, therefore, differs considerably from that of Old Testament prophets. See *Body Builders* for further clarification.

With these things in mind, as we now turn to 1 Corinthians 14, it should be clear that it's the gift of prophecy and possibly the ministry of prophets that Paul is talking about.

The value and purpose of prophecy

Returning now to 1 Corinthians 14, as we read verse 1 it becomes immediately clear that Paul valued prophecy very highly indeed. He says that we should *eagerly desire* it:

> *Follow the way of love and eagerly desire spiritual gifts, especially the gift of prophecy.*

This is the main theme of the chapter. He ends the chapter as he has started it:

> *Therefore, my brothers, be eager to prophesy...*(39).

The Greek word Paul uses for *eagerly desire* is very strong. It's the origin of our English word *zeal.* God wants us to *be passionate about* prophecy. Notice that in verse 1 Paul doesn't say **or**. He says **and**.

> *Follow the way of love **and** eagerly desire spiritual gifts.*

The pursuit of spiritual gifts is not an optional extra. We must not say, *I have love, so I don't need spiritual gifts.* We must eagerly desire spiritual gifts, and *especially the gift of prophecy* (1). But why?

The value of the gift is to be seen in its purpose. We should be passionate about prophecy because it edifies the church. Paul says in verses 4 and 5:

> *... he who prophesies edifies the church. I would rather have you prophesy... so that the church may be edified.*

What he means by this is explained in verse 3 where he says:

> *But everyone who prophesies speaks to men for their **strengthening, encouragement and comfort**.*

In the context of church worship this is the practical outworking of Paul's teaching about love in chapter 13. We are to love our fellow Christians, and if we love them we will want to be a blessing to them, to strengthen, encourage, and comfort them. And that's what prophecy does.

But that's not all. Prophecy can also have a powerful effect on unbelievers who may come into the church. In Chapter Five we discussed some of the difficulties in understanding verses 22-23, but verses 24-25 are very clear:

> *But if an unbeliever or someone who does not understand comes in while everybody is prophesying, he will be convinced by all that he is a sinner and will be judged by all,*
>
> *25 and the secrets of his heart will be laid bare. So he will fall down and worship God, exclaiming, "God is really among you!"*

So prophecy is to be valued very highly, not only because it strengthens, encourages, and comforts believers, but also because of the powerful effect it can have on people who do not yet believe. But having said that, prophecy is not without its limitations. In 13:9-10 Paul says:

> *For we know in part and we prophesy in part, 10 but when perfection comes, the imperfect disappears.*

This is because at present our knowledge is incomplete. W*e see but a poor reflection as in a mirror* (12). Our prophecies are *imperfect* because they are *our* prophecies, and we are not perfect yet. That's why in 14:12 Paul tells us to *try to excel* in it. If our use of God's precious gifts were perfect, we would not need to try to excel in them – in fact all Paul's instructions about their use would have been unnecessary! And that's why we're told in 14:29 that we should *weigh carefully what is said.* But that brings us to how prophecy should be used in church.

The use of prophecy in church

Perhaps the first thing to say about the use of prophecy in church is that we should always bear in mind its purpose, which is to strengthen, encourage, comfort, and edify God's people (3-4). There is no suggestion that it should be used to rebuke them, or even to give them guidance.

Paul tells us in Romans 8:14 that it's our privilege as God's children to be personally led by the Spirit. Guidance received through prophecy should simply serve as **confirmation of something that God has already spoken to us** about in our hearts. A good example of this is found in Acts 13:1-3 where the prophets and teachers in the church at Antioch were told by the Holy Spirit to set Barnabas and Paul apart for the work to which he had **already** called them[24].

So, bearing in mind the purpose for which the gift of prophecy is given, we are now in a position to consider Paul's specific teaching on the use of the gift in church. This is found in verses 29-32 where he says:

---

[24] See also Paul's attitude to the prophecy of the prophet Agabus in Acts 21:1-15. Agabus predicts what will happen to Paul, but he does not tell him what to do.

29 Two or three prophets should speak, and the others should weigh carefully what is said. 30 And if a revelation comes to someone who is sitting down, the first speaker should stop. 31 For you can all prophesy in turn so that everyone may be instructed and encouraged. 32 The spirits of prophets are subject to the control of prophets.

Two or three prophets should speak (29)

Note the contrast with verse 27. Paul does not say *if* with regard to prophecy. It is not merely to be permitted but to be encouraged. The prophets *should* speak. But how is Paul using the word *prophet* here? Is he talking about prophets like Agabus, the kind of ministry he refers to in Ephesians 4:11, or does he mean those who exercise the simple gift of prophecy?

Some have suggested that *two or three prophets should speak* in verse 29 refers to those with the ministry of a prophet (as in Ephesians 4:11), but that when Paul says in verse 31 *you can all prophesy* he is referring to the whole church. However, the use of the word *for* in verse 31 clearly identifies the people he is speaking to as the prophets he addresses in verses 29-30. This means that verses 29-31 must all refer to the same people, either those who are prophets, or those who have the gift of prophecy, or even to both.

Although we cannot say with certainty which group Paul is addressing in these verses, it is very clear that the principles he is teaching apply to both. The first of these is that although prophecy is to be encouraged its use is to be limited and it needs to be judged or weighed carefully.

The others should weigh carefully what is said (29)

The verb translated *weigh carefully* is the same as is used for distinguishing between spirits in 12:10. The clear implication is that every prophecy needs to be evaluated, and this illustrates the point that we made earlier that it is by no means infallible. However, despite its limitations, Paul tells us in 1 Thessalonians 5:19-20 that it's not to be despised. But even that may indicate the possibility of human weakness in the operation of the gift, for why else would the Thessalonians have been despising it?

So prophecy needs to be judged or weighed carefully. But this raises two questions. The first is: **Who** *is responsible for judging it?* Looking at the immediate context, Paul seems to mean the other *prophets*. The things of the Spirit are spiritually discerned (2:14), and those with a prophetic gift are more likely to accurately weigh a prophetic revelation.

But surely *the others* may be applied more widely than that? As we have seen, there is a sense in which all God's people are prophets, and we all have the capacity, and the responsibility, to weigh prophetic words. And certainly those who are pastors or teachers have a special responsibility to be alert for anything that might mislead the flock.

Secondly, we need to consider the question: **How** *is prophecy to be judged?* There are two areas of importance here, its *authenticity* and its *application*. By *authenticity* I mean its conformity to Scripture. Paul is very clear in verse 37 that *what (he is) writing... is the Lord's command*. All prophecy must be judged in the light of what the Spirit has already said in the Bible.

By *application* I mean that we need to consider to whom the prophecy may apply. Is it for me? Is it for the whole church? How do we apply it in practice? These are decisions that we all must make after hearing a prophecy. Clearly, we cannot judge it until we have heard it! However, in some churches people who feel they have a prophetic word to bring are expected to share it with the church leadership before bringing it publicly. The church leaders evaluate it before it is given. The advantages of this are twofold:

- It prevents any unauthentic or inappropriate prophecy being given in public.

- Those who are inexperienced, but eager to prophesy, feel more secure in having their prophecy confirmed by the leaders before bringing it.

However, it's surely unthinkable that those with a proven track record in prophecy should have to consult the church leaders before they prophesy. Their prophecies should be judged *after* they have delivered them, which is almost certainly what Paul intended. Furthermore, the insistence that leaders must be consulted before prophecies are given seems out of keeping with the encouragement Paul gives in verse 26 for all to participate, and with the spontaneity implicit in his teaching on the matter in verse 30.

And if a revelation comes to someone who is sitting down, the first speaker should stop (30)

This not only shows the spontaneity that Paul envisages; it also shows that, although the purpose of prophecy is mainly the strengthening, encouragement, and comfort of the church, it may also contain an element of revelation. It also seems to suggest that it was the custom to stand when prophesying while others were seated. Perhaps the second person would stand to indicate that they had received a revelation from the Spirit and that is how the first person would know it was time to stop. Be that as it may, the important point here is that each prophet must be prepared to make room for others who exercise the gift.

For you can all prophesy in turn so that everyone may be instructed and encouraged (31)

What does Paul mean when he says, *You can all prophesy?* In my view this cannot possibly refer to all the congregation, as this would contradict the principle taught in chapter 12 that the gifts are distributed as the Spirit determines and would be out of harmony with the phrase *to **another** prophecy* (12:10).

Taken in context he must surely mean that all the prophets, or all those with the gift of prophecy, may prophesy. Each person must be given opportunity to exercise their gift as the Spirit may lead, but presumably not in contravention of the *two or three* principle of verse 29.

The spirits of prophets are subject to the control of prophets (32)

It seems likely that by *spirits* here Paul is referring to their *spiritual gift.* While the Greek word *pneuma* normally means *spirit*, Paul does use it in 14:12 to refer to spiritual gifts, when he says, *Since you are eager to have spiritual gifts, try to excel...* Understood this way, verse 32 means that the spiritual gift of prophecy is under the control of the person who exercises it.

Indeed, all the gifts that God gives us are under our control. This is clear from the fact that specific instructions are given for their use. If the use of the gifts were only dependent upon the Holy Spirit himself such instructions would be both inappropriate and unnecessary. And because of our responsibility for the control of the gift God has given us, as we have already seen, Paul teaches that we are able to:

- regulate the number of prophetic utterances in any one meeting (14:29).
- cease prophesying if something is revealed to someone else (14:30).
- prophesy rather than speak in tongues if unbelievers are present (14:23-25).

Our ability to control the gift of prophecy also implies that we are responsible for the terminology in which we express the message that God has given us. Since we are not infallible, we would be wise to phrase our prophecies in the **third person** rather than the first, to talk of God as *he* and not *I*. For example, it would be better to say

The Lord loves you...

than to say, '

I love you, says the Lord.

We may believe that God has given us something to say, but we are not God, and we should not talk as if we were!

But that now brings us to the final verses of 1 Corinthians 14. As our subject in this chapter has been Paul's teaching on the gift of prophecy, We will confine our attention to those verses that are directly relevant to this subject. Verses 34-35 in the NIV read as follows:

> *34 women should remain silent in the churches. They are not allowed to speak, but must be in submission, as the Law says. 35 If they want to inquire about something, they should ask their own husbands at home; for it is disgraceful for a woman to speak in the church.*

It is clear that in the context silence is relative and not absolute. The exhortation relates to asking their husbands questions at home (35) and not to worship or exercising spiritual gifts such as prophecy. In fact we read in 11:5 that Paul permitted women to both pray and prophesy in church, and although it's possible to pray silently, it's certainly not possible to prophesy silently!

> *37 If anybody thinks he is a prophet or spiritually gifted, let him acknowledge that what I am writing to you is the Lord's command. 38 If he ignores this, he himself will be ignored. 39 Therefore, my brothers, be eager to prophesy, and do not forbid speaking in tongues. 40 But everything should be done in a fitting and orderly way.*

As he draws to his conclusion Paul summarises his teaching on public worship in a few short verses. Whatever your spiritual gift may be you must submit to the authority of the apostle's commands (37). This has obvious implications with regard to the authority of Scripture, but also to the authority of ministry gift over spiritual gifts. Prophecy is to be encouraged and tongues should not be forbidden (39). Whatever happens, everything should be done in a fitting and orderly way.

CHAPTER EIGHT

Identifying Underlying Principles

We have now completed our examination of 1 Corinthians 12-14 with a view to seeing how Paul's teaching in those chapters might help us better understand the verse upon which this book is based, 1 Corinthians 14:26. In our consideration of chapter 12 we saw from the first part of the chapter that we should expect the supernatural gifts of the Holy Spirit in our meetings and that the baptism in the Holy Spirit is the gateway to those gifts.

In the second part of the chapter, we highlighted the principles of unity, diversity and interdependence. The different gifts we have are all given by the same Spirit, and we all belong to the same body. Every part of the body is important, and every part needs each other part.

The chief lesson that we learnt from chapter 13 is that nothing that we have and nothing that we may do is of any value without love. We also saw that, wonderful though they are, supernatural gifts have their limitations. They are neither permanent nor perfect. *We know in part, and we prophesy in part.* And that's because *that which is perfect* has not yet come.

In chapter 14 we discovered that most of Paul's teaching is taken up with the value and use of the gifts of tongues, interpretation, and prophecy, and so we devoted the last three chapters to discussing what Paul teaches about each of these gifts in that chapter. We looked in some detail at his specific instructions and sought to clarify their meaning where that was open to possible differences of interpretation and application.

With all these things in mind, we now return to 1 Corinthians 14:26 to consider in more detail some of the things we outlined in the Introduction.

> *What then shall we say, brothers? When you come together, everyone has a hymn, or a word of instruction, a revelation, a tongue or an interpretation. All of these must be done for the strengthening of the church.*

The first thing to remember about this verse is that Paul is giving guidance on what should happen in a meeting of believers. This is clear from the overall context, from the use of the words *brothers... when **you** come together,* and from verse 24 where he says ***if** an unbeliever comes in.* So I am not suggesting that the principles taught in this verse should be applied to an evangelistic meeting, for which his recommendations might have been different.

Secondly, as I pointed out in the Introduction, the words, *What then shall we say, brothers?* indicate that what follows contains a recommendation. Clearly this is crucial to all that I am arguing in this book, but my confidence is based on Paul's use of the same Greek phrase in verse 15 where it's clear that Paul is making a strong recommendation.

Thirdly, in the Introduction we identified three key principles in this verse:

- Participation
- Variety
- Edification.

We will now explore these concepts in more detail.

Participation

Paul hardly needed to *recommend* that the Corinthians participate in their meetings. That was something they were doing already. Verse 23 seems to suggest that there were occasions when they were all speaking in tongues at the same time and this was something Paul wanted to discourage, especially in the presence of unbelievers. This is why he felt the need to limit speaking in tongues to two, or at the most, three.

The problem was not lack of participation, but too much participation in things that did not edify the church. So verse 26 is both a recognition and a recommendation – a recognition of what was already happening, and a recommendation that whatever that was, it should be done for the strengthening of the church.

But to say this is not to minimise the importance of the whole verse as a recommendation to *us*. Referring to the things he has listed in the verse, Paul says, **All of these** must be done. And they must be done *for the strengthening of the church.* As we saw from chapter 12, every part of the body is needed. There should always be opportunity, whenever we gather, for the expression of the many gifts and graces that the Spirit has imparted to the members.

Of course, it would not be possible in most churches for every person present to participate in every meeting, other than to join in singing the songs and, perhaps to say an occasional *Amen* to what is being said by others. But there should always be *opportunity* for them to do so.

And they should be *encouraged* to do so. People are more likely to participate when time is specifically allocated for this, and when it's made clear that participation is welcome. If we really want people to participate, we must make room for it, even if it means arranging smaller meetings, or, in larger meetings, breaking down into small groups for part of the service.

But, as I said in the Introduction, it's not my intention to try to tell church leaders what they should do. If we really believe that the things that Paul has written in this chapter are *the Lord's command* (37), we will find ways of implementing them that will work in our particular situation.

Variety

Paul refers to:

> *a hymn, or a word of instruction, a revelation, a tongue or an interpretation.*

These are, of course, just a representative sample of what might happen in a meeting, but they suggest three main areas:

- The musical dimension (*a hymn*)
- The doctrinal dimension (*a word of instruction*)
- The supernatural dimension (*a revelation, a tongue,* etc).

We have already dealt with the supernatural dimension at some length. So we will confine our attention to the musical and doctrinal dimensions.

The musical dimension

The first thing Paul refers to in 14:26 is *a hymn*. Actually the word in Greek is literally a *psalm*. A psalm has been defined as a song or poem used in worship, so the translation *hymn* is quite appropriate. Of course, at the time Paul was writing to the Corinthians they would not have had the vast repertoire of hymns and songs that are available to us today.

However, because of the Jewish origins of the Christian church, it's likely that their main source of songs for worship would have been the Book of Psalms that we have in our Bible. In fact, where the word *psalm* is used everywhere else in New Testament it refers to one of the Psalms, so this is probably what Paul had in mind when he said:

Everyone of you has a hymn (or psalm).

But what exactly did Paul mean by this? Although we cannot be sure how this recommendation would have been applied in Corinth, there is one clear implication in what Paul is saying. Everyone should have the opportunity to contribute to the worship by *having* a song. But how do you *have* a song? This surely means more than joining in the songs chosen in advance by the pastor or worship leader! And Paul is hardly suggesting that everyone should have the opportunity to sing a solo, wonderful though the ministry in song of Christian vocal artists may be.

In my view, the most appropriate way of implementing Paul's recommendation within the context of modern worship is to give opportunity for people to choose a hymn for everyone to sing, or, in a time of open worship, to spontaneously start singing a well-known hymn or chorus for everyone to join in.

I realise that this may not easily fit in with modern styles of worship where the pursuit of excellence in performance seems to be paramount, but I know from experience what a blessing it can be when someone in the congregation spontaneously *has a song* in one of the ways I have just suggested.

Finally, with reference to the songs we sing, may I make two pleas to Christian song writers? First, with regard to the melodies, would you please compose those that are quickly learned, easily remembered, and easily sung by members of the congregation who don't have your musical expertise or vocal range? The recent trend of pitching songs in keys that only seem to suit the worship leader's voice really does not serve the congregation well.

And secondly, please remember that the words of a song are more important than the music. Music is valuable, not only because it helps us express our emotion and lifts our spirit, but also because it helps us *remember* what we sing. So it's important that our words clearly express in easily understood English the great truths of our faith. Your songs have the potential to be remembered far more than my sermons! So please make sure you've got your theology right, and, if you're not sure, get someone else to check it for you. In fact, don't be afraid to include some weighty theological truths in your writing – historically many hymns were written in order to teach doctrine!

Finally, we need to consider the only other reference to singing in 1 Corinthians 14, where in verse 15, talking about singing in tongues, Paul says:

> *I will sing with my spirit (in tongues), but I will also sing with my mind (in a language I understand).*

However, as we have already seen, this is part of what Paul is recommending for the use of tongues in private, which raises the question as to whether singing in tongues is appropriate in public. There may be a reference to this in Ephesians 5:19 where Paul mentions *spiritual songs* along with psalms and hymns. KJV is more literal than NIV when it translates this as

> ***speaking* to *yourselves*** *in psalms and hymns and **spiritual songs**, singing and making melody in your heart to the Lord...*

We know from 1 Corinthians 14 that speaking in tongues is one way of speaking to ourselves and to God (28) and that in doing so we are praying or singing with our spirit (14-15). However, it's unclear whether, in Ephesians 5:19, Paul is envisaging a public or private situation. The reference to *heart* rather than *hearts* might suggest that he is speaking to them as individuals, whereas *speaking to yourselves* (plural) could be taken to refer to when they are gathered in worship.

Perhaps he intends both. At Pentecost the disciples were filled with the Spirit both collectively and individually and we need, both as a church and as individuals within it, to keep on being filled with the Spirit. If I can sing in tongues privately to maintain the fulness of the Spirit, cannot the church do so collectively? I confess that I was once rather concerned about this, especially when unbelievers were present, on the basis of what Paul says about them thinking we are mad (14:23). But the following episode made me think again.

During part of the time when I was Principal of Mattersey Hall Bible College, the college chapel was across the road from the main part of our campus, and the students' worship could easily be heard by anyone passing by. There would often be times when everyone was spontaneously singing in tongues to worship the Lord, and I wondered what the local residents might think of it. But I was greatly reassured when I heard that one of them had asked:

> *What is that beautiful singing I sometimes hear when I walk past your chapel? It's so unusual, and it gives me a great sense of peace.*

The Corinthians were undoubtedly out of order in the way they were exercising the gift of tongues and clearly needed the strong warning that Paul gave them. But perhaps today he might be encouraging some churches at least to move in the opposite direction and be less concerned about what outsiders might think. As at Pentecost, there will always be those who criticise the moving of the Spirit, but if we are able to give an explanation of what's happening, as Peter did, there may well be more who are persuaded by our message than those who oppose it.

The doctrinal dimension

The Greek word translated in NIV as *a word of instruction* is *didache*, which literally means *teaching*. It can also mean *doctrine* (which comes from a Latin verb meaning *teach*). Paul says relatively little about this in 1 Corinthians 14, but in verse 19 he stresses the importance of teaching when he says:

> *But in the church I would rather speak five intelligible words to **instruct** others than ten thousand words in a tongue,*

and in verse 31 when he says:

> *For you can all prophesy in turn so that everyone may be **instructed** and encouraged.*

And of course, as we mentioned in the Introduction, most of the contents of Paul's letters were written to instruct the churches in the truth and to expose false doctrine. As I have said elsewhere,

> What we believe is of vital importance. The scriptures were written that we might *know the truth*, and that the truth might set us free (John 8:32). Every genuine experience of the Spirit finds its foundation in the truth of God's word. The

Bible is the inspired word of God. It teaches the truth – about God, about man, about life and death, good and evil, heaven and hell. If we want to know the truth about any of the important questions of life, we will find it in the Bible[25].

John tells us that

> *Anyone who… does not continue in the teaching of Christ, does not have God. Whoever continues in the teaching has both the Father and the Son* (2 John 9).

Jesus himself told his disciples to beware of the teachings of the Pharisees (Matthew 16:12) and said that their teachings were just rules made by men (Matthew 15:9), and Paul warns us of the same danger in Colossians 2:22. But what a wonderful contrast is *the teaching of God our Saviour* (Titus 2:10) which is to be recognised by a right attitude to Christ (2 John 7-10) and a right attitude to scripture (2 Timothy 3:16).

We need to know *what* we believe and *why* we believe it so that we can *by sound doctrine convince those who contradict us* (Titus 1:9). It is by knowing the truth that people are set free (John 8:32). That's why Paul told Timothy:

> *Devote yourself to… teaching. Watch your life and doctrine closely; persevere in them; because if you do you will save both yourself and your hearers* (1 Timothy 4:13, 16).

---

[25] Introduction to *You'd Better Believe it*. This book contains teaching on the basic doctrines of the Christian faith and is available from www.davidpetts.org.

The sound exposition of the Scriptures is essential whenever we come together.

Edification

We said at the beginning of the chapter that the three key principles underlying 14:26 are participation, variety, and edification. Now that we have discussed the first two of these, we turn to the subject of edification, which, without doubt is the major theme of the whole chapter. If love is the dominant theme of chapter 13, in chapter 14 edification is the way that love is expressed in the context of the gathered church. That's why Paul says everything *must be done for the strengthening of the church.*

We have already looked at Paul's specific teaching in chapter 14 in some detail, but now it will be helpful to consider the key principles that underly that teaching and see if they can be applied more widely than the specific issues Paul was addressing in Corinth. As we do so, we will discover five principles that need to be applied if our meetings are to be edifying.

Putting other people first

This is the principle underlying Paul's teaching in verses 1-5. There he is saying that in church prophecy is more valuable than tongues because when you speak in tongues you edify only yourself, but if you prophesy you will edify others. He picks up the same theme in verse 17:

> *You may be giving thanks well enough, but the other person is not edified.*

The principle underlying this teaching is putting others first. And that principle can be applied far more widely than the issue of speaking in tongues. For example, it's good that I have the freedom to stand and worship the Lord while others are sitting down, but if by standing I prevent the person behind me from singing because they cannot see the words on the screen in front, I may be giving thanks well, but the other person is not edified. People need to be taught to be considerate to others in the way they worship the Lord.

Intelligibility

Another of the ways we can build up our fellow Christians is by making sure they can *understand*. In verse 9 Paul says:

> *Unless you speak **intelligible** words with your tongue, how will anyone know what you are saying?*

Of course, he's talking about the futility of speaking in tongues in church unless it's interpreted. It's pointless unless people can **understand** it. But that's true of everything we do in church. Not everything we say in English is easy to understand – but it should be! This applies to our preaching, our prayers, the songs we sing, our praise and worship – everything. In verse 16 it's clear that Paul expects that everyone present should be able to say *Amen* to whatever we say, but to do that they must first *understand* it,

> *…how can one who… does not understand say "Amen" to your thanksgiving, since he does not know what you are saying?*

Again, in the context, he's talking about speaking in tongues, but the underlying principle of intelligibility has a wider application. For example, how can I say *Amen* to someone's prayer or praise if I can't make out what they're saying because the people around me are making too much noise, or if the background music is too loud?

Which, incidentally, it often is. Saying *Amen* means expressing your agreement with what's been said, and you can't do that if you haven't heard it properly.

Responsibility

As we saw in the last chapter when discussing prophets and prophecy, Paul says that

> *The spirits of prophets are subject to the control of prophets* (32).

This implies that both prophets and those who have the gift of prophecy are responsible for how they use their gifts. But the need to take responsibility for our actions goes far wider than the gift of prophecy. If God has entrusted us with any spiritual gift, we are responsible for how we use it.

For example, the Holy Spirit does not *force* us to speak in tongues. He *enables* us to do so. We are responsible for when, how often, and how loudly. This principle applies to everything we do in church. We are to follow the teaching of Scripture and of our leaders (37-38) and we cannot make the excuse, *I couldn't help it. The Holy Spirit made me do it.* And, as we have already said, the very fact that Paul gave us instructions on how these gifts should be used implies that we are responsible for how we use them.

Order

Paul says that *God is not a God of disorder but of peace* (33), and it's our responsibility to see that *everything is done in a fitting and orderly way* (40). In the context this meant ensuring that speaking in tongues should be done *one at a time* and that only *one person* should interpret each utterance (27). And the same principle applied to the use of prophecy (30).

Paul's specific teaching on this is still applicable today, but the wider principle holds good for everything we do. **Everything** *should done in a fitting and orderly way.* Interpretation of what is *fitting and orderly* will possibly vary from church to church, and there will undoubtedly be cultural variations, but the leaders of each church should be able to agree on what is appropriate in their situation, bearing in mind the overall principles taught in Scripture.

Balance

Finally, it's clear from Paul's teaching that there needs to be a measure of balance in our meetings. In Corinth there was too much speaking in tongues. In another church it might be too much music, or even too much teaching! If there is to be the variety of which Paul speaks in verse 26, and if each member is to have the opportunity to contribute, church leaders need to ensure that there is a healthy balance in each meeting.

But that is not to say that there cannot be special occasions when an entire meeting is given over to teaching, or to prayer, or to worship, for example. Such occasions are not to be confused with the regular meetings of the church, where preserving a measure of balance will be essential to the edification of all God's people.

So, to summarise, in this chapter we have examined the three principles underlying Paul's teaching in 1 Corinthians 14:26 – participation, variety, and edification. We noted that our meetings should include the supernatural, the musical and the doctrinal. But, most important of all, we saw that everything should be done for the edification of the church, and that this will be achieved by putting others first, making sure that what is said is intelligible, taking responsibility for our actions, and by preserving order and balance in our meetings. These principles have a wider application than the specific areas that Paul was addressing in the Corinthian church. Exactly how they should be applied is for each local church leadership to decide. And that is something we will be discussing in our next and final chapter.

CHAPTER NINE

Putting it all into practice

As we now turn to suggesting how we can put Paul's teaching into practice, it will be important first to consider exactly who is responsible for doing so. And, as we look again at 1 Corinthians 14:26, it becomes immediately apparent that the verse is addressed to *everyone* in the church:

> *What then shall we say brothers and sisters? When you come together, **everyone** has…*

So everyone has a responsibility in this matter. But that raises the important question of the role of church leaders. What exactly is their responsibility? In *Body Builders,* I have discussed the role of church leaders in some detail[26]. There we noted that their responsibilities include shepherding the flock, instructing them in the truths of God's word, and managing and directing the affairs of the church (1 Timothy 3:5, 5:17).

Applying these principles to 1 Corinthians 14:26, this clearly implies that, apart from any other duties they may have, church leaders have a special responsibility in ensuring that what Paul teaches is put into practice whenever Christians come together to worship the Lord. If church members are to fulfil their responsibility to participate in the meetings as Paul teaches in 14:26, church leaders will need to encourage them to do so. The purpose of this chapter is to offer some guidance as to how they might do this.

---

[26] See especially the chapter on *Pastors.*

Being fully persuaded in your own mind

Now that you have almost finished reading this book, the time has come for you to make up your mind. I encourage you to read again chapters 12-14 of 1 Corinthians and especially consider what implications 14:26 might have for your church. In Romans 14:5, Paul wrote:

Let everyone be fully persuaded in their own mind.

Although written in a different context, this principle is of vital importance in every area of our Christian living. We must take care that we are not *tossed back and forth by the waves and blown here and there by every wind of teaching* (Ephesians 4:14).

This is particularly relevant in situations where the implementation of a 14:26 style of worship could be controversial. Change often makes people feel uncomfortable, and some of them will probably tell you so. But, if you are fully persuaded in your own mind that this is what God says, you will be able to bear criticism patiently and in time, hopefully, to persuade them of the truth. That's why it's especially important to pray for guidance.

Praying for guidance

In making these suggestions on how we might lead our church into a more biblical way of doing things, I am well aware that every situation is different. Apart from the obvious denominational differences in styles of worship and leadership, there are sometimes very different ways of doing things, even in churches of the same denomination. That's why, I have placed prayer for guidance high on our list of priorities.

Once we have grasped the truth of God's word on the matter, we need to pray for guidance on how and when we should introduce these things. When seeking to introduce any form of change where there has been a well-established tradition, I have personally always felt it wise to take things slowly and only introduce the change after teaching clearly why the change is both biblical and necessary. But that's something for the leaders of each local church prayerfully to decide together. Which leads us to our next point.

Consulting your fellow leaders

As mentioned in the last section, I realise that different churches have different forms of leadership. Although I am personally persuaded that team leadership should be the aim of every local church, it's not my intention to argue the point here, as I have already done so at some length in *Body Builders.* However, I would suggest that, even in churches where there is only one leader, it would be wise for that leader to consult with key people in the church before seeking to implement any major changes in the style of worship.

On the other hand, where there is already an established pastoral team, it's important that each pastor or elder is committed to the principle of 14:26 meetings and that the team agrees on how it should be applied in their local situation. Decisions need to be made not only on how and when to introduce it, but also on how to interpret and apply Paul's teaching, particularly where there is legitimate room for different ways of understanding what he is saying.

I have listed on the next page some of the issues it would be wise to consider. I have already expressed my own opinion on these matters, but it's for each leadership team to make their own decision. The sort of things I'm referring to are:

a) With regard to speaking in tongues when unbelievers come in, should there be:

>No tongues at all?

>Tongues only if it's for interpretation?

>Everybody speaking in tongues?

b) With regard to the gift of interpretation of tongues:

>Should this sound like praise or prophecy?

>What does *Someone must interpret* mean (v. 27)?

>Should a fourth utterance in tongues be interpreted?

>Should private tongues be interpreted?

c) With regard to the gift of prophecy:

>How many? 2 or 3? Or no limit?

>How do you judge it? Who should judge it?

>How do you apply v.30?

>>*And if a revelation comes to someone who is sitting down, the first speaker should stop.*

Once you have decided these issues you will need to teach them to the people. But there will be other areas where teaching will be needed too.

Teaching the people

I have discovered from years of experience that *you get what you teach for.* Jesus said, *You will know the truth, and the truth will set you free* (John 8:32). God's people are released into freedom when they know the truths of God's word. Few will be saved if we do not preach the gospel. Few will be healed if we do not preach about healing. And the same applies to the baptism and gifts of the Holy Spirit, which are essential if our meetings are to follow the biblical pattern of 1 Corinthians 14:26.

It is vital that when people become Christians they are encouraged to receive the baptism in the Holy Spirit as soon as possible after their conversion (Acts 2:38). This gives them an early introduction into the charismatic dimension of life in the Spirit. And, of course, they must be taught to keep on being filled with the Spirit on a daily basis (Ephesians 5:18, 2 Timothy 1:6).

And once people have been filled with the Spirit, it's important that they receive teaching on spiritual gifts. It's important that we give clear guidelines for the use of the gifts (as Paul did in 1 Corinthians 12-14). This way the people feel the security of knowing how and when they may be appropriately exercised. That's why we need to have decided in advance what our policy will be about the issues mentioned in the last section.

We must encourage people to exercise the gifts and lovingly correct them where necessary. Because we're human, our use of the gifts is not infallible. People will make mistakes. But if these are corrected lovingly and sensitively, the whole congregation will feel secure under a firm but caring leadership, and those who are beginning in the gifts can learn to excel so that the church might be built up (1 Corinthians 14:12).

Finally, we need to remember that the best way to teach is by setting an example. We need not only to tell people what they should do, but, equally importantly, to show them how to do it. Some of the fastest growing churches in the world are churches where the leadership sets the example in the use of spiritual gifts. However, it's important that leaders do not give the impression that they are the only ones that God can use in the exercise of these gifts. The purpose of setting an example is, after all, to encourage others to do the same.

Making space

And if we really want to encourage people to participate in our meetings, we must make space for them to do so. We have already acknowledged that it will be difficult to put into practice the principles taught in1 Corinthians 14:26 in a large gathering, but there is no good reason why space could not be made available for people to participate for at least a part of the meeting.

Another way to make such participation possible would be to ask the congregation to break into groups of, say, seven to ten people and encourage them to share together for perhaps twenty minutes or so. I once did this after teaching for six Sunday mornings on 1 Corinthians 12-14. I encouraged everyone to say at least something that might be a blessing to others, even if it was just a favourite verse of Scripture or the verse of a hymn. And I was pleased to hear afterwards how grateful the people were to have been given the opportunity to do so.

You might also consider arranging some special *'14:26 meetings'* either on a Sunday or during the week. This could be a useful way of gradually introducing a congregation, who have been unused to it, to this style of worship. If you decide to do this it would be wise to tell people in advance what you're going to do and to come prepared to participate.

And of course, an obvious setting for this kind of meeting would be in home groups. However, before attempting to do so, home group leaders might well need training and teaching the principles we have already discussed. You could perhaps take your homegroup leaders together through the teaching, giving them opportunity to experience and practise what they've learnt.

Creating a suitable environment

Finally, it's vital that we provide the right environment for the gifts to flourish. If as leaders we seek to create an atmosphere of love in the church, people will not be afraid to move forward in faith. In the right kind of spiritual atmosphere spiritual gifts flow naturally and easily. It is not difficult to have the faith to prophesy in a fellowship where believers love each other and want to edify one another and where the leaders will sympathetically encourage us and, if necessary, lovingly correct us as we seek to move forward in faith.

Conclusion

My purpose in writing this book has been to show that we should take seriously Paul's teaching in 1 Corinthians 14:26 and encourage a greater measure of Spirit-led congregational participation in our meetings. We have acknowledged that the things that Paul wrote are *the commandments of the Lord* (14:37), not just for the Christians in first century Corinth, but for us today.

In order to put 1 Corinthians 14:26 in context, and to understand more fully what Paul is saying in this verse, we have examined chapters 12-14 in some detail and have seen that there's a supernatural dimension to the worship of the church expressed in the manifestation of supernatural gifts given by the Holy Spirit (12:1-11) and that these all spring from our being baptised in the Spirit (12:13), which is an experience promised by Jesus and described by Luke in the Book of Acts.

We saw that Paul's teaching that the church is the body of Christ, that every member of the body is different, and that everybody is needed (12:12-30), undergirds his recommendation in 14:26 that everyone should have opportunity to contribute to the meeting.

Furthermore, his teaching that everything we do must be motivated by love (13:1-13) and that, as an expression of that love, we must always seek to put other people first (14:1-25), impinges directly on how the principles taught in 14:26 should be applied in practice. This will mean, among other things, using correctly the spiritual gifts God has given us by taking responsibility for our actions (14:26-40).

In this connection, we examined carefully Paul's teaching on tongues, interpretation, and prophecy in chapter 14, as these are the subjects he concentrates on in that chapter and are specifically mentioned in 14:26. We sought to clarify the meaning of verses that are open to differences of interpretation and to suggest how they might be applied in practice, acknowledging that in everything we must submit to the authority of scripture (14:37).

Finally, in this chapter we have offered some guidelines as to how all these things might be put into practice. Church leaders have a special responsibility in this, and, as I have said more than once already, it is not my intention to tell leaders what they should do – that is their responsibility under God. But it is my sincere prayer that what I have written may be of some help in bringing our meetings closer to God's revealed will for what should happen when we come together.

Other helpful books by David Petts

The Holy Spirit – an Introduction

For a detailed look at the person and work of the Holy Spirit this book is a must. It deals with the Spirit in the Old and New Testaments, the Spirit in the teaching of Jesus, the Spirit in the believer, the fruit and gifts of the Spirit, the Spirit in the church, and the Holy Spirit in the future.

Body Builders – gifts to make God's people grow

A detailed look at spiritual gifts in the New Testament, examining particularly the gifts listed in Ephesians 4:11 and those in 1 Corinthians 12:8-10. This book will help you understand what these gifts are, how to receive them, and how to use them.

Signs from Heaven – why I believe

A short book intended as an evangelistic tool containing testimonies of miracles from my own experience.

Just a Taste of Heaven – a biblical and balanced approach to God's healing power

As the title suggests, this book is about healing. Part One deals with biblical passages on healing. Part Two presents a positive but balanced theology of healing and Part Three offers practical guidelines for ministering to sick people with examples of miracles of healing from my own experience. If you want to be used in healing, I encourage you to read this book.

You'd Better Believe It!

20 chapters on basic Christian doctrine with study questions at the end of each chapter. Suitable for personal study or for use in home-groups.

How to Live for Jesus

Intended for new Christians, this book contains 10 short chapters on living the Christian life.

The Voice of God – How he speaks to us today

This book is about how God *speaks* and how he *guides* us. It will help you to recognize his voice, to know when he is speaking to you and when he is not.

A New Dimension – How to be filled with the Holy Spirit

A short book giving clear teaching on the baptism in the Holy Spirit and how to receive it.

For more details on any of these books

and

for further copies of this book, visit:

www.davidpetts.org

A series of podcasts to accompany this book is also available.